The Two-Sector
General Equilibrium Model
A NEW APPROACH

The Two-Sector General Equilibrium Model

A NEW APPROACH

C. L. Dinwiddy & F. J. Teal

Philip Allan / St. Martin's Press

First published 1988 by

PHILIP ALLAN PUBLISHERS LIMITED
MARKET PLACE
DEDDINGTON
OXFORD OX5 4SE

First published in the USA 1988 by

ST. MARTIN'S PRESS, INC.
SCHOLARLY AND REFERENCE DIVISION
175 FIFTH AVENUE
NEW YORK, N.Y. 10010

British Library Cataloguing in Publication Data

Dinwiddy, C.L.
    The two-sector general equilibrium model:
    a new approach.
    1. Equilibrium (Economics) —— Mathematical
    models
    I. Title   II. Teal, F.J.
    330.15'43   HB145

    ISBN 0–86003–072–5
    ISBN 0–86003–175–6 Pbk

Library of Congress Cataloguing-in-Publication Data

Dinwiddy, Caroline L.
    The two-sector general equilibrium model : a new approach / C.L.
    Dinwiddy and F.J. Teal.
        p.   cm.
    Bibliography: p.
    Includes index.
    ISBN 0–312–01877–0 : $30.00 (est.)
    1. Equilibrium (Economics)   I. Teal, F. J.   II. Title.
    HB145.D56 1988
339.5– –dc 19   87–36935
                                                              CIP

Typeset by Photoprint, Torquay
Printed and bound in Great Britain by The Alden Press, Oxford

CONTENTS

PREFACE

The idea that all markets in an economy are linked together, and that changes in one market will typically have repercussions in some or all the other markets for goods and factors, is referred to, but is not usually developed in any systematic way, in introductory economics courses. The important step from partial to general equilibrium analysis is normally postponed to intermediate courses where students are likely to encounter the two-sector model of general equilibrium. This model is widely used for teaching international trade theory and, following the approach of H.G. Johnson (1971), the same framework is now used for presenting a wide range of topics from welfare economics, the theory of public finance, the theory of economic growth and general equilibrium analysis. The two-good, two-factor model has the obvious advantage that it can be studied using two-dimensional graphs, and it is by means of diagrams and geometric techniques that the two-sector model typically contributes to economic analysis.[1]

Although the diagrammatic presentation of the two-sector model has proved a very useful tool in the above fields, it does not provide a wholly satisfactory basis for the formal study of general equilibrium models in their own right. The vision of the economy as a vast system of interlocking markets was first expounded by Leon Walras (1834–1910) using sets of simultaneous equations to describe the necessary conditions for equilibrium in the product and factor markets. Two strands in contemporary economic literature derive from the work of Walras. At an advanced theoretical level economists have been working on problems concerning the existence and the nature of a competitive general equilibrium and, on the applied side, developments in computing

---

1. At undergraduate level, a comprehensive introduction to the two-sector model and its applications using this approach can be found in Baldry (1980). For international trade theory see, for example, Krauss (1977); and for an example of an intermediate microeconomic textbook which bases much of its analysis on the two-sector model, see Layard and Walters (1978).

1

have led to the construction of computable general equilibrium models which can be used for forecasting and policy analysis.[1]

Despite the importance of these recent developments in economic analysis, it is often difficult for students at an undergraduate or first-year graduate level to find a simple introduction to the construction of a general equilibrium model. Almost all students of economics are now offered courses in elementary mathematics covering differentiation, an introduction to optimisation theory, and methods of solving systems of simultaneous equations. However, these techniques are rarely employed to show how a model of general equilibrium is formulated. The reason for this would appear to be that although the equations of the model can be constructed using tools familiar to most second-year undergraduate students, even the very simple example of a two-sector model introduced in Chapter 1 comprises a system of 15 equations in 15 unknowns; and until recently, the solution of such a system would have been virtually impossible. Without a means for solving the system much of the point of setting up the equations of the model would be lost.

With the advent of the microcomputer this situation has changed. Any small personal computer can be programmed to 'search' for an equilibrium solution to a system of equations. Writing a program to solve a general equilibrium model provides in itself some insight into the nature of the general equilibrium system. Such a program can be used to do more than provide a solution to the model; once written, the program can become the basis for 'experiments' which enable the general equilibrium consequences of economic change to be analysed. To take one example, the effects of an increased supply of one factor of production on levels of production, consumption and relative prices can be examined. Other 'experiments' can show the effects of the imposition of a tariff in an economy which previously enjoyed free trade, or the relative welfare consequences of different forms of Government intervention in the economy. To conduct these 'experiments', which show the consequences of a change in an economic variable for all the markets of an economy, a fully formulated general equilibrium model is required.

The 'new' approach referred to in the title of this book consists of

---

1. For an example from each of these two fields, students could look at Arrow (1983), and Dervis, De Melo and Robinson (1982).

a full presentation of the two-sector general equilibrium model in terms of a complete system of equations, together with a discussion of the procedures for solving such a system using a microcomputer and suggestions for using the computer programs as a basis for economic analysis. The approach may be thought of as an extension of the partial equilibrium models familiar to any student of economics, in which each market is described by a supply equation, a demand equation and an equilibrium condition. In general equilibrium the supply and demand functions in both product and factor markets will typically be related to *all* the prices in the system, and the income and expenditure relations of all the economic agents in the economy — firms, households, Government — have to be explicitly modelled.

There are a number of advantages in such an approach to the two-sector model. In the first place, it makes explicit in a way that two-dimensional diagrams cannot, the way in which all markets and all agents are linked together in an economy. It is complementary to the traditional approach in that familiar results from the theory of international trade and elementary propositions in welfare economics can be demonstrated by the use of appropriate models. In addition, some concepts peculiar to the theory of general equilibrium, such as the use and interpretation of Walras' Law (which often puzzles students even at graduate level), can be very clearly illustrated by the use of specific examples. More importantly, this approach to general equilibrium models can readily be generalised in a way that the diagrammatic approach cannot. It is straightforward to enlarge the model from a two-good model to one with three or more commodities. Chapter 8 of this book discusses the ways in which the basic two-good model can be extended, and we include a brief account of an n-commodity model used to examine the effects of the Canadian import tariff. In this way, the foundations are laid for the study of the large-scale empirical general equilibrium models. It is a large step from two- and three- good models to models such as the ORANI model of the Australian economy with its 113 industries and 230 commodities, and the extensions into econometrics which are required for the construction of empirical models are not part of this book; but the student who has worked through the present text would have some insight into the nature of the task.

The book is organised in the following way: Chapter 1 discusses the nature of economic models and introduces the equations of the simplest two-good, closed-economy general equilibrium model; Chapter 2 provides a specific numerical example of this model, discusses the formal properties of such a model and shows how the system of equations can be solved by means of a BASIC computer program. The remaining chapters build on this approach. The basic model is extended first by a discussion of the implications of constant returns to scale, then by the incorporation of foreign trade, and finally by the explicit inclusion of a public sector. In each case, the general model is illustrated by a specific numerical example which can be used to demonstrate the workings of a general equilibrium system; and the later models are used to illuminate some propositions from international trade theory. Those who are only interested in the structure of simple general equilibrium models could omit the numerical examples, but the 'do-it-yourself' aspects of the computer experiments seem to us to offer students of economics a powerful insight into many of the formal propositions of economic theory.

References

Arrow, K.J. (1983) *General Equilibrium*, Vol. 2, in the *Collected Papers of Kenneth J. Arrow*, Basil Blackwell.

Baldry, J.C. (1980) *General Equilibrium Analysis, An Introduction to the Two-sector Model*, Croom Helm.

Dervis, K., De Melo, J. and Robinson, S. (1982) *General Equilibrium Models for Development Policy*, a World Bank Research Publication, Cambridge University Press.

Johnson, H.G. (1971) *The Two-sector Model of General Equilibrium*, George Allen and Unwin.

Krauss, M.B. (1977) *A Geometric Approach to International Trade*, Basil Blackwell.

Layard, P.R.G. and Walters, A.A. (1978) *Microeconomic Theory*, McGraw-Hill.

NOTATION

The same notation has been used for the variables of all the two-sector general equilibrium models in Chapters 1 – 7. The following table lists the variables and gives both the algebraic notation and the equivalent variable names used in the BASIC computer programs. (A few variables appear only in the BASIC programs.)

VARIABLE	ALGEBRAIC NOTATION	BASIC VARIABLE NAME
PRIVATE SECTOR DEMAND AND SUPPLY		
Demand for good 1	C_1	C1
Demand for good 2	C_2	C2
Supply of good 1 by firm 1	X_1	X1
Supply of good 2 by firm 2	X_2	X2
Demand for capital by firm 1	K_1	K1
Demand for capital by firm 2	K_2	K2
Demand for labour by firm 1	L_1	L1
Demand for labour by firm 2	L_2	L2
Per unit demand for capital by firm 1	k_1	UK1
Per unit demand for capital by firm 2	k_2	UK2
Per unit demand for labour by firm 1	l_1	UL1
Per unit demand for labour by firm 2	l_2	UL2
Fixed endowment of capital	$K^\star$	K
Fixed endowment of labour	$L^\star$	L
Total use of capital by private sector	–	KX
Total use of labour by private sector	–	LX
PUBLIC SECTOR PRODUCTION		
Public sector production of good 1	G_1	G1
Public sector production of good 2	G_2	G2
Public sector demand for capital	Kg	KG
Public sector demand for labour	Lg	LG
DOMESTIC PRICES		
Price of good 1	P_1	P1
Price of good 2	P_2	P2
Consumer price of good 1 (when different from producer price)	Q_1	Q1

Consumer price of good 2
(when different from producer price) Q_2 Q2
Rental on capital r R
Wage rate w W

TAXES
Commodity tax t_C TC
Import tariff t_M TM
Lump-sum (income) tax t_Y TY

FOREIGN SECTOR
Exports E E
Imports M M
Exchange rate F F
Balance of Payments –   BP
World price of good 1 P_{W1} PW1
World price of good 2 P_{W2} PW2

PRIVATE AND PUBLIC SECTOR
INCOME
Consumer's income Y Y
Profits of firm 1 Π_1 PI1
Profits of firm 2 Π_2 PI2
Government revenue from production G G
Government revenue from taxation T T
Public sector budget –   PSB

1
THE EQUATIONS OF A GENERAL EQUILIBRIUM MODEL

1.1 What is a General Equilibrium Model?

The concept of 'equilibrium' is one of the first encountered by students of economics. An individual market is said to be in equilibrium when the quantity of a good demanded is equal to the quantity supplied. This will occur when the equilibrium price prevails; that is, when the price at which suppliers are prepared to sell a given quantity is equal to the price at which consumers desire to buy the same amount. If the price lies above the equilibrium level there will be excess supply; if the price lies below the equilibrium there will excess demand; in either of these cases the market is said to be in disequilibrium. The underlying hypothesis of competitive market behaviour is that excess supply will cause price to fall and excess demand will cause price to rise, so that in any competitive market the price is always tending towards its equilibrium level.

The above analysis is known in economic theory as static partial equilibrium analysis. It is static because the element of time is ignored and it is partial because the analysis relates to price changes in only one market. In this book we do not consider the problems that can arise when moving from static to dynamic analysis; but we do consider the consequences of moving from partial to general equilibrium analysis.

General equilibrium analysis deals explicitly with the inter-relationships between different markets and different sectors of the economy. While the concepts of general equilibrium are not usually studied formally at an introductory level, every first-year student of macroeconomics is familiar with the concept of the circular flow of income. In the simplest model of the economy, where there is no saving or investment, no government and no foreign trade, the circular flow is as shown in Figure 1.1. On the right-hand side of

7

the diagram are the commodity markets in which the goods and services produced by the firms are purchased for consumption by the households; on the left-hand side are the factor markets in which factor services are supplied by households to the firms in exchange for factor payments. These factor payments represent the income of the households which is then available for consumers to

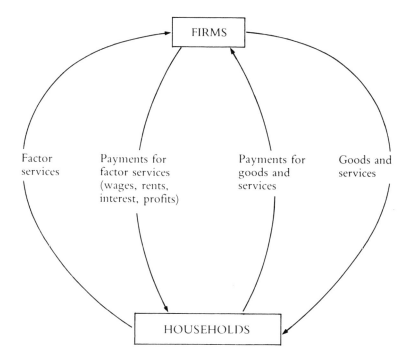

Figure 1.1 The Circular Flow of Income

spend in the commodity markets; the expenditure on goods and services constitutes the income of the firms. If there are m commodity markets and n factor markets there will be altogether $m+n$ markets and $m+n$ equilibrium prices to be determined if each market is to be in equilibrium. When all markets are in equilibrium, the economy is said to be in a state of general equilibrium.

The construction of a model describing an economy in which all markets are in equilibrium requires a set of equations describing supply, demand and equilibrium conditions for each of the $m+n$

markets of the economy, and equations specifying the income of each economic agent in the economy; the economic agents in the simple model represented by Figure 1 are the firms and the households. Before discussing these equations in detail, we consider what is meant by an economic model.

1.2 Models, Equations and Variables

Models are a formal presentation of some aspect of economic theory using the language of mathematics; the hypothesised relations between variables are represented by an equation or a set of equations. Models are widely used in advanced economic analysis and it is essential for any student wishing to proceed beyond an introductory level in economics to become familiar with the ways in which models are formulated and used. An early introductory work in this field justified this approach in the following terms:

> It is not claimed that the whole of economics or even the whole of economic theory can be encompassed in a model or a set of models. But it is claimed that a well-devised model can bring out certain features of interdependence among economic quantities that are not easily comprehended without its help. It makes the assumptions more precise, the relationships more evident, and allows the theory to be tested for logical consistency. (Beach, 1957)

All of these aspects of model construction will be stressed in the presentation of the two-sector general equilibrium models of this text.

The equations of a model may simply be general statements of functional relationships between economic variables, or the equations may be given a specific functional form. An example of a general statement of a model would be the partial equilibrium model

$$Q^D = Q^D(P) \qquad dQ/dP < 0$$
$$Q^S = Q^S(P) \qquad dQ/dP > 0$$
$$Q^D = Q^S$$

where Q^D represents the quantity of a good demanded, Q^S the quantity supplied, and P the price. This model includes two behavioural equations describing the hypothesis made about the way in which the demand for the good and the supply of a good are related to its price, and one equation defining the equilibrium condition for the market. A specific example of the above model is

$$Q^D = 100 - 2P$$
$$Q^S = -10 + 3P$$
$$Q^D = Q^S$$

In this case the constant terms in the equations, known as the parameters of the model, determine the exact relationship between P and Q in the two behavioural equations. When the equations are specified in this way it is possible to solve the model for the equilibrium values of the variables; in the latter example it is easy to show that the equilibrium value of P is 22, and the equilibrium value of Q is 56.

One of the most important questions to be considered when setting up an economic model is the question of which variables are to be treated as endogenous to the model, i.e. variables whose value is to be determined by the solution to the system of model equations, and which variables are to be exogenous, taking values determined outside the model. In the market models considered above, all the variables Q^D, Q^S, and P are endogenous — the simultaneous system can be solved for the equilibrium values of all three variables. Suppose however that, for example, the supply of an agricultural product is thought to be affected by the number of centimetres of rain falling during the growing season, and let this variable be represented by R. The model would then have the general form

$$Q^D = Q^D(P) \qquad dQ^D/dP < 0$$
$$Q^S = Q^S(P,R) \qquad dQ^S/dP > 0 \qquad dQ^S/dR > 0$$
$$Q^D = Q^S$$

There are three endogenous variables, Q^D, Q^S, and P; and one exogenous variable, R. The specific form of the model might be given by

$$Q^D = 100 - 2P$$
$$Q^S = -10 + 3P + 0.5R$$
$$Q^D = Q^S$$

and in order to find the equilibrium values of the endogenous variables it would be necessary to 'plug in' a value for the exogenous variable R, which could be ascertained from meteorological records.

It is not always so obvious which variables in a model should be treated as endogenous and which exogenous. Rainfall is clearly not an economic variable. However, the model could include an income variable (Y) in the demand function. In a partial equilibrium model such as the one being considered, household income is usually treated as an exogenous variable, and if for example the specific form of the demand function became

$$Q^D = 100 - 2P + 0.01Y$$

values for Y could be supplied exogenously from household income data, and the model could be solved as before for equilibrium values of the endogenous variables. In another model it might not be appropriate to treat income as exogenous. If, for example, the model was intended to represent the market for rice in a small Asian village, the income as well as the expenditure of the peasant producers would clearly be affected by the rice price, and the model would have to be redesigned with a new equation incorporating this relationship; the equilibrium values of P and Q would then simultaneously determine the equilibrium value of Y, and the income variable would have become endogenous. The decision to treat a variable as exogenous or endogenous is taken by the model-builder in view of the economic relationships of immediate interest. In the general equilibrium models with which we are concerned in this book, it is evident from a glance at the circular flow diagram that the income of the households and firms are determined by the prices and quantities prevailing in the product and factor markets. These interrelationships have to be made explicit by the inclusion of equations defining the income relations of the households and firms as well as the equations describing market equilibrium.

An essential point to be borne in mind in the construction of economic models is that a system of equations will not, in general, have a unique solution unless there are as many equations as there are unknowns. This means that any number of exogenous variables can be added to a model if they are thought to be appropriate, but if a new endogenous variable is added, a new equation defining the way in which the new variable fits into the system must also be added.

1.3 The Equations of a Two-sector General Equilibrium Model

In this section we discuss the equations necessary to describe the general equilibrium system of a very simple two-sector economy.

There are assumed to be two goods, each produced by one of the two firms in the economy using two factors of production — capital and labour. We assume that the factor endowments are fixed and that both are owned by a single household. By making the assumption that there is only one representative household, we rule out for the time being any discussion of distribution issues. However, many propositions in the theory of international trade and public policy can be considered using a one-consumer general equilibrium model, and we return in Chapter 7 to a discussion of the questions that arise when more than one household is included in the analysis.

As discussed above, the general equilibrium model must specify the demand and supply relations and the equilibrium condition for each market, and must also include a specification of the income constraint of each of the economic agents in the economy; in this simple economy there are three economic agents — the two firms and the single consumer.

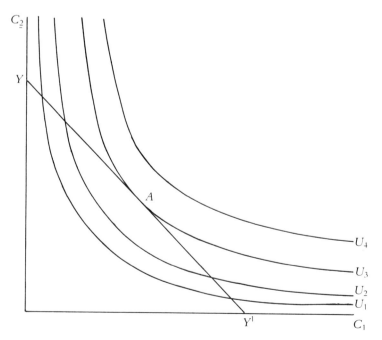

Figure 1.2 Maximisation of the Consumer's Utility Subject to a Budget Constraint

We begin by considering the commodity markets. Using the subscripts 1 and 2 to denote the two goods, the quantities of the two goods supplied are represented by X_1 and X_2 and the consumer's demand is represented by C_1 and C_2. The two prices are denoted by P_1 and P_2. For each market we shall have three equations: a supply equation, a demand equation, and a market clearing equation (often referred to in the general equilibrium literature as a commodity balance equation).

The nature of the demand and supply functions is dictated by economic theory. The consumer is assumed to maximise utility subject to a budget constraint which states that the household's total expenditure on the two goods must equal the consumer's income (Y). If the utility function is assumed to be concave, the indifference curves will be convex, and the maximisation problem

Maximise $\quad U = U(C_1, C_2)$
subject to $\quad P_1 C_1 + P_2 C_2 = Y$

can be represented by the familiar diagram of Figure 1.2 where U_1, $U_2, \ldots$ are the isoquants of the utility function and YY represents the budget constraint. The graphical solution to this problem is represented in Figure 1.2 by the point A where the budget line is tangential to the isoquant showing the highest level of utility that can be achieved. From the solution to the consumer's constrained optimisation problem come the demand relations

$$C_1 = C_1(P_1, P_2, Y) \tag{1.1}$$
$$C_2 = C_2(P_1, P_2, Y) \tag{1.2}$$

showing that consumption depends upon commodity prices and income. (A specific numerical example of the derivation of demand functions is given in the next chapter.)

The derivation of the supply functions is based on a two–stage optimisation procedure. In the first place, a firm employing two factors of production capital (K) and labour (L) will require certain combinations of the two factors to produce a given level of output. The relationship betwen inputs and output is given by the production function which for firm i takes the general form

$$X_i = X_i (K_i, L_i)$$

where K_i and L_i are the quantities of capital and labour used by firm i. The costs of production will be determined by the factor prices, denoted here by r for the price of capital and w for the price of labour, and the least-cost combination of the factors will be found from the solution to the cost-minimisation problem

minimise $TC_i = rK_i + wL_i$
subject to $X_{io} = X_{io}(K_i, L_i)$

where TC_i represents the total costs of firm i and X_{io} is the desired level of output. This problem can be represented graphically by the diagram of Figure 1.3, where the isoquant X_{io} shows the desired

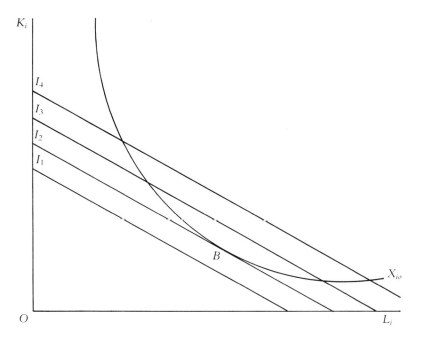

Figure 1.3 Minimisation of a Firm's Costs for a Given Level of Output

level of output and the slope of the isocost lines I_i is determined by the relative factor prices. In this diagram B represents the least-cost combination of factors.

The firm's short-run supply function will now be determined by a second optimisation procedure: each firm is assumed to maximise its profits, defined as the difference between its total revenues (TR_i) and its total costs (TC_i) as illustrated in Figure 1.4.

In Figure 1.4, X_{io} is the profit-maximising level of output, determined for firm i by the price at which it sells its product P_i,

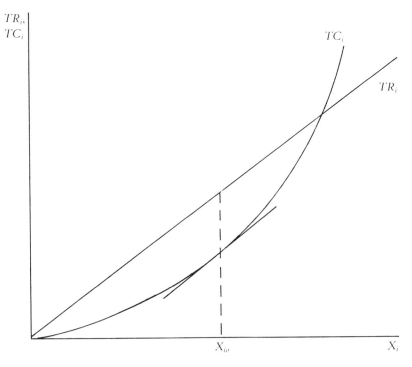

Figure 1.4 Maximisation of a Firm's Profits

and by the costs of production which, as we have seen, are determined by the factor prices r and w. The general form of these supply functions is therefore described by equations (1.3) and (1.4). (Again, specific numerical examples of the derivation of supply functions are provided in the next chapter.)

$$X_1 = X_1(P_1,w,r) \tag{1.3}$$
$$X_2 = X_2(P_2,w,r) \tag{1.4}$$

Equations (1.1) – (1.4) describe the demand and supply functions for the two commodities in this simple two-sector economy. For equilibrium in the product markets we must add the market clearing equations

$$C_1 = X_1 \tag{1.5}$$
$$C_2 = X_2 \tag{1.6}$$

Next we consider the factor markets. The demand for each factor comes from the solution to the firm's cost-minimisation problem discussed above, and illustrated in Figure 1.3. Given the desired profit-maximising level of output each firm will employ the corresponding cost-minimising quantities of the two factors of production which, as we have seen, will be determined by the factor prices. We have therefore the following functions relating the demand for factors by each firm to the chosen level of output X_i, and the factor prices r and w:

$$K_1 = K_1(X_1, w, r) \tag{1.7}$$
$$K_2 = K_2(X_2, w, r) \tag{1.8}$$
$$L_1 = L_1(X_1, w, r) \tag{1.9}$$
$$L_2 = L_2(X_2, w, r) \tag{1.10}$$

In a more complex model the supply of factors to each firm by the consumer would be derived from the household preference set and the relative prices in the system, but in the simple model we are considering it is assumed that the total quantity of capital available is fixed exogenously at $K^\star$ and the total quantity of labour is fixed at $L^\star$. The factor market clearing equations therefore take the form

$$K_1 + K_2 = K^\star \tag{1.11}$$
$$L_1 + L_2 = L^\star \tag{1.12}$$

The twelve equations (1.1) – (1.12) give the conditions for equilibrium in the commodity and factor markets. The general equilibrium system is not however complete because the income equations for the firms and the household have still to be considered. Each firm will make profits (which we denote by Π_i) equal to the difference between its total revenue from the sale of its product, and its expenditure on factor inputs. We have therefore

$$\Pi_1 = P_1 X_1 - wL_1 - rK_1 \tag{1.13}$$
$$\Pi_2 = P_2 X_2 - wL_2 - rK_2 \tag{1.14}$$

Finally, the consumer's income Y has to be defined. In this stylised one-consumer economy, the single consumer not only supplies the factor services, but is also the sole shareholder in the economy, and receives the profits of the two firms. The income of the consumer is therefore defined by the following equation:

$$Y = w(L_1 + L_2) + r(K_1 + K_2) + \Pi_1 + \Pi_2 \tag{1.15}$$

The general equilibrium system is complete. It consists of 15 equations in the following 15 endogenous variables: $C_1, C_2, X_1, X_2,$ $K_1, K_2, L_1, L_2, P_1, P_2, w, r, \Pi_1, \Pi_2, Y$. In addition there are the two exogenous variables $K^\star$ and $L^\star$. Given appropriate functional forms for the demand and supply functions (1.1) – (1.4) and (1.7) – (1.10) it will be possible to solve for all the equilibrium quantities produced and consumed in the commodity and factor markets. It will also be possible to establish the relative prices, though not the absolute price level, that will prevail at equilibrium. These issues are discussed further in the next chapter where a specific numerical example of the above model is considered.

It will be seen that although formulating models of 15 equations in 15 unknowns is not a usual approach to economic analysis at the introductory level, the concepts involved are all familiar from first-year undergraduate courses. The advantage of approaching these topics from a general equilibrium viewpoint is that it prepares the way for a study of the all-important links between markets. To take one example, it is clear that if for some reason — a change in immigration policy perhaps — the supply of labour L^* alters, market equilibrium will require a change in the wage rate w. The new value for w will affect all the other equilibrium relationships in the system; factor demands alter, and so do the levels of output X_1 and X_2. The consumer's income is affected by the change in w and so therefore is the household demand for the two commodities C_1 and C_2. New values for the relative prices P_1 and P_2 will emerge and these will in turn lead to further shifts in the patterns of supply and demand. These interrelationships will be explored further by means of the specific numerical example introduced in the next chapter.

References

Beach, E.F. (1957) *Economic Models*, John Wiley and Sons.

2
THE TWO-SECTOR MODEL: A NUMERICAL EXAMPLE

2.1 Introduction

In this chapter we construct a specific numerical example of the closed economy two-sector general equilibrium model formulated in Chapter 1. The construction of a specific model shows very clearly what assumptions have to be made before a full set of general equilibrium equations can be derived, and the solution to such a model can be used to demonstrate some of the characteristics of a general equilibrium system. Sections 2.2 and 2.3 show how, given specific assumptions about the form of the consumer's utility function and the firms' production functions, demand and supply functions can be derived. The mathematics required for the analysis of these two sections is an elementary knowledge of constrained optimisation procedures. This subject is covered in most introductory mathematics textbooks written for students of economics, and the relevant concepts are summarised in an Appendix at the end of this chapter. (For a more comprehensive treatment of constrained optimisation, students are referred to the texts listed at the end of the book under the heading 'Suggestions for Further Reading'.) The full model is summarised in Section 2.4, and in Section 2.5 the meaning and use of a numeraire and the workings of Walras' Law are discussed. Solving a large system of nonlinear simultaneous equations necessitates the use of a computer, and the last section of the chapter includes a simple BASIC program which can be written and run on any small personal computer. The model developed in this chapter and the specific example of the constant returns to scale model developed in Chapter 4 are used as the basis for all the other numerical examples in the book, and once written, the BASIC programs for the closed economy models can easily be adapted to solve the models incorporating the foreign sector introduced in Chapter 5 and the public sector introduced in Chapter 6.

2.2 The Derivation of Demand Functions

Household demand functions can be derived from the solution to the consumer's constrained optimisation problem. The general form of this problem was discussed and illustrated in Figure 1.2 in the previous chapter. For specific demand functions, an assumption has to be made about the form of the consumer's utility function. For our two-good model we assume that the consumer maximises

$$U = C_1^{1/2}C_2^{1/2} \tag{2.1}$$

subject to

$$P_1C_1 + P_2C_2 = Y \tag{2.2}$$

where, as before, C_1 and C_2 are the quantities of the two goods consumed, P_1 and P_2 are their prices, and Y is the consumer's income. Using the Lagrange multiplier technique outlined in the Appendix to this chapter we formulate the Lagrangean for the problem

$$Z = C_1^{1/2} C_2^{1/2} + \lambda(P_1C_1 + P_2C_2 - Y)$$

and the first-order or necessary conditions for an optimum are given by

$$\frac{\delta Z}{\delta C_1} = \frac{\delta Z}{\delta C_2} = \frac{\delta Z}{\delta \lambda} = 0,$$

yielding the following three equations to be solved for the utility-maximising values[1] of C_1, C_2 and λ:

$$\frac{1}{2} C_1^{-1/2}C_2^{1/2} + \lambda P_1 = 0 \tag{2.3}$$

$$\frac{1}{2} C_1^{1/2}C_2^{-1/2} + \lambda P_2 = 0 \tag{2.4}$$

$$P_1C_1 + P_2C_2 - Y = 0 \tag{2.5}$$

Each of the equations (2.3) and (2.4) can be solved for λ in terms of

---

1. With the functional forms assumed for the utility function and the firms' production functions in this chapter, the second-order conditions needed to distinguish between maximum and minimum values can be taken for granted. See the Appendix for further discussion of this point.

the other variables and if the two resulting expressions are equated
we find

$$\frac{P_2}{P_1} = \frac{C_1}{C_2} \tag{2.6}$$

from which

$$P_2 = P_1 \frac{C_1}{C_2} \tag{2.7}$$

Substituting for P_2 in (2.5) from (2.7) gives

$$P_1 C_1 + P_1 C_1 = Y$$

and this equation can be solved for the demand function for good 1:

$$C_1 = \frac{Y}{2P_1} \tag{2.8}$$

Similarly, solving equation (2.6) for P_1 and substituting for P_1 in
(2.5) gives the demand function for good 2:

$$C_2 = \frac{Y}{2P_2} \tag{2.9}$$

(2.8) and (2.9) represent the household demand functions for
commodities 1 and 2 respectively. We refer to demand functions
rather than demand curves because (2.8) and (2.9) are expressions
showing the relationship between the quantity demanded of the
good on the one hand, and its price and the consumer's income on
the other. The textbook demand curve concentrates on the quantity
demanded/price relationship and subsumes the income effect in the
ceteris paribus assumption, but the use of mathematics makes
possible a fuller representation of important relationships in
economic theory. The reader will find it a useful exercise to
calculate the partial derivatives $\delta C_i / \delta P_i$ and $\delta C_i / \delta Y$, and the
elasticities for each of the two demand functions in order to show
that, as economic theory requires, demand responds negatively to
changes in price and positively to changes in income.

It will be apparent that the derivation of specific demand
functions in the manner described above requires the assumption
that information about the form of the consumer's utility function
is available, and the reader may well question the realism of this
assumption. Utility functions are clearly not observable
phenomena. However, much recent microeconomic theory has

been concerned with the possibility of inferring underlying utility functions from observable data on prices and incomes. With this approach, empirical data are used to derive demand relationships and the economic theorist looks for demand functions which are compatible both with the available evidence and with the restrictions on the possible forms of demand functions which are imposed by utility theory. The construction of an empirical, as opposed to a purely theoretical, general equilibrium model would start with the observable evidence and work backwards to the hypothesised utility function. In this text we have for simplicity used a Cobb-Douglas function of the general form

$$U = C_1{}^\alpha C_2{}^\beta$$

Other forms are possible; one that has been extensively explored using empirical data is that underlying the so-called linear expenditure system:

$$U = \Sigma \alpha_i \log(C_i - \beta_i)$$

where C_i is the consumption of the ith commodity and α_i and β_i are parameters of the utility function. Readers interested in this area of analysis could look at Deaton and Muellbauer (1980) for an extensive discussion of the issues involved.

2.3 The Derivation of Supply Functions

As discussed in Section 1.3 of the previous chapter, the derivation of supply functions for a firm in a perfectly competitive industry is a two-stage procedure. First the firm has to determine the quantities of each factor it will employ for any given level of output. These quantities will then determine its (minimum) total cost for each level of output. Having determined the total cost function the firm can then formulate its profit maximisation problem which consists of choosing that level of output which maximises the difference between total revenue and total cost.

We consider first the cost minimisation problem for firm 1 in our two-sector economy. The firm is assumed to employ given quantities of two factors of production, capital (K_1) and labour (L_1), at prices represented respectively by r and w. The solution to the cost minimisation problem will enable us to derive factor demands (and hence an expression for total costs) for any level of output (X_1). The general problem was represented graphically by

Figure 1.3; in order to formulate a specific problem, an assumption has to be made about the form of the firm's production function. We assume that the production function has the specific form

$$X_1 = K_1^{1/4} L_1^{1/2} \tag{2.10}$$

This production function is of the general Cobb–Douglas form $X = K^\alpha L^\beta$. The Cobb–Douglas production function has been widely used in the estimation of empirical relationships.[1] Some other ways of modelling production are discussed in the following chapter.

Using TC_1 to represent the firm's costs, the problem is to minimise

$$TC_1 = rK_1 + wL_1 \tag{2.11}$$

subject to the production function (2.10). (2.10) can be solved for L_1 in terms of X_1 and K_1 to give

$$L_1 = \frac{X_1^2}{K_1^{1/2}} \tag{2.12}$$

and substituting (2.12) for L_1 in (2.11) enables us to formulate the (unconstrained) minimisation problem

$$\text{minimise } TC_1 = rK_1 + w\left(\frac{X_1^2}{K_1^{1/2}}\right)$$

From this expression we can derive the demand for the factor of production K_1 (capital), for any level of output X_1. The first-order condition for a minimum is given by $dTC_1/dK_1 = 0$, yielding the equation

$$r - \frac{wX_1^2}{2K_1^{3/2}} = 0 \tag{2.13}$$

which can be solved for K_1 in terms of the level of output X_1 and the factor prices r and w:

$$K_1 = \left(\frac{wX_1^2}{2r}\right)^{\frac{2}{3}} \tag{2.14}$$

This function, relating firm 1's demand for capital to its level of

1. See Hebden (1984) for a discussion of the properties of the Cobb–Douglas production function, and a number of empirical studies using this relation.

output and factor prices, is known as the conditional demand for capital of firm 1. In a similar way we can solve (2.10) for K_1 giving

$$K_1 = \frac{X_1^4}{L_1^2} \tag{2.15}$$

and by substituting for K_1 in $TC_1 = rK_1 + wL_1$ (equation 2.11) and minimising TC_1 with respect to L_1 we derive the conditional demand for labour by firm 1:

$$L_1 = \left(\frac{2rX_1^4}{w}\right)^{\frac{1}{3}} \tag{2.16}$$

The first stage in the derivation of the firm's supply function is now complete. Equations (2.14) and (2.16) tell us the quantities of the factors of production, capital and labour, that will be demanded for any given values of r, w, and X_1. The next stage is to formulate the firm's profit function and then determine the profit-maximising level of output X_1. Profits are the difference between total revenue and total cost for any level of output X_1. If we represent the price of the product of firm 1 by P_1, the total revenues of the firm (TR_1) will be given by

$$TR_1 = P_1 X_1$$

Total costs are given by $TC_1 = rK_1 + wL_1$, and by substituting the conditional demands for capital and labour given by (2.14) and (2.16):

$$TC_1 = r\left(\frac{wX_1^2}{2r}\right)^{\frac{2}{3}} + w\left(\frac{2rX_1^4}{w}\right)^{\frac{1}{3}}$$

so that the profit function $\Pi_1 = TR_1 - TC_1$, showing Π_1 as a function of X_1 is given by

$$\Pi_1 = P_1 X_1 - r\left(\frac{wX_1^2}{2r}\right)^{\frac{2}{3}} - w\left(\frac{2rX_1^4}{w}\right)^{\frac{1}{3}} \tag{2.17}$$

The profit-maximising level of output is found by setting the derivative $d\Pi_1/dX_1 = 0$, giving the equation

$$P_1 - \frac{4}{3}w^{2/3}r^{1/3}X_1^{1/3}\left[2^{1/3} + \left(\frac{1}{2}\right)^{2/3}\right] = 0 \tag{2.18}$$

to be solved for X_1. The solution is

$$X_1 = \frac{P_1{}^3}{16w^2r} \qquad (2.19)$$

(2.19) is the supply function for firm 1, showing quantity supplied in terms of the price of the product P_1 and the prices of the factors of production r and w. The partial derivatives of the function show that, as economic theory would predict, quantity supplied responds positively to an increase in the price of the product, and negatively to increases in the price of its factors of production.

To derive factor demands and a supply function for the second firm in the two-good economy, firm 2, we assume a production function of the form

$$X_2 = K_2{}^{1/2}L_2{}^{1/4} \qquad (2.20)$$

which by the same cost-minimising and profit-maximising operations as those worked through for firm 1 yields the two factor demand equations

$$K_2 = \left(\frac{2wX_2{}^4}{r}\right)^{\frac{1}{3}} \qquad (2.21)$$

$$L_2 - \left(\frac{rX_2{}^2}{2w}\right)^{\frac{2}{3}} \qquad (2.22)$$

and the supply function

$$X_2 = \frac{P_2{}^3}{16r^2w} \qquad (2.23)$$

where X_2 represents the level of output of firm 2, K_2 and L_2 represent respectively the demands for capital and labour by firm 2, and P_2 represents the price of the output of firm 2 in the product market.

Although working through the algebra required to derive demand and supply functions may seem a laborious process, it is worth emphasising how much has been achieved. Using only the concepts of optimisation and constrained optimisation, and the appropriate mathematical procedures, the reader has been able to follow through a great many of the fundamental concepts of neo-classical micro-economics and the relations between them. Demand functions, relating quantity demanded to price and income, have been shown to depend upon the nature of the consumer's utility function and the household budget constraint; supply functions, relating supply to product price and factor prices, have been shown to depend upon the nature of the production function and the firm's cost constraint. Furthermore, the demand for factors of production by the firm has been related to the firm's cost minimisation exercise and shown to depend upon both the level of output and factor prices.

No further algebra is required to formulate a complete general equilibrium system for the two-sector economy with the consumer's utility function and the firms' production functions assumed above, and in the next section we set out the full set of equations and then proceed to discuss the manner in which the system can be solved for the equilibrium values of all the endogenous variables.

2.4 The Equations of the Model

Table 2.1 sets out a specific version of the general equilibrium system described by equations (1.1) – (1.15) in the previous chapter. In Table 2.1 the equations (1.1) and (1.2) have been replaced by the specific demand functions (2.8) and (2.9) derived above; equations (1.3) and (1.4) have been replaced by the specific supply functions derived above as equations (2.19) and (2.23); and the factor demand functions (1.7) – (1.10) are represented by (2.14), (2.16), (2.21) and (2.22). The remaining equations of the model describing the market clearing conditions and the budget constraints of the consumer and the firms are unchanged.

2.5 The Need for a Numeraire and Walras' Law

There are two properties peculiar to general equilibrium models which must be discussed before we can proceed to write the computer program to solve the above system. In the first place, it is necessary to consider the proposition that in a general equilibrium model it will not be possible to determine the absolute price level: only relative prices can be established. This proposition reflects the well-known fact that if *all* prices increase in the same proportion, but relative prices are unaltered, the real relationships in the

Table 2.1 A Numerical Example of a Closed Economy Model

COMMODITY MARKETS

Demand

$$C_1 = \frac{Y}{2P_1} \tag{1}$$

$$C_2 = \frac{Y}{2P_2} \tag{2}$$

Supply

$$X_1 = \frac{P_1{}^3}{16w^2 r} \tag{3}$$

$$X_2 = \frac{P_2{}^3}{16r^2 w} \tag{4}$$

Market clearing

$$C_1 = X_1 \tag{5}$$

$$C_2 = X_2 \tag{6}$$

FACTOR MARKETS

Demand

$$K_1 = \left(\frac{wX_1{}^2}{2r} \right)^{\frac{2}{3}} \tag{7}$$

$$K_2 = \left(\frac{2wX_2{}^4}{r} \right)^{\frac{1}{3}} \tag{8}$$

$$L_1 = \left(\frac{2rX_1{}^4}{w} \right)^{\frac{1}{3}} \tag{9}$$

$$L_2 = \left(\frac{rX_2{}^2}{2w} \right)^{\frac{2}{3}} \tag{10}$$

Market clearing

$$K_1 + K_2 = K^\star \tag{11}$$
$$L_1 + L_2 = L^\star \tag{12}$$

INCOME EQUATIONS

Firms

$$\Pi_1 = P_1 X_1 - rK_1 - wL_1 \tag{13}$$
$$\Pi_2 = P_2 X_2 - rK_2 - wl_2 \tag{14}$$

Consumer

$$Y = r(K_1 + K_2) + w(L_1 + L_2) + \Pi_1 + \Pi_2 \tag{15}$$

The 15 endogenous variables are $\quad C_1 \; C_2 \; X_1 \; X_2 \; K_1 \; K_2 \; L_1 \; L_2$
$$P_1 \; P_2 \; w \; r \; \Pi_1 \; \Pi_2 \; Y$$

The variables $K^\star$ and $L^\star$ are exogenous.

economy remain unchanged. This can be demonstrated by considering a familiar example from elementary microeconomics. Suppose a household has an income of 100 which is spent on two goods, C_1 with price 10 and C_2 with price 20. The household can have 10 units of C_1 and no C_2; 5 units of C_2 and no C_1; or it can purchase some combination of C_1 and C_2 determined by the relative prices of the two commodities. Now suppose the price level doubles: the household's income increases to 200, the price of C_1 is 20, and the price of C_2 is 40. It is easy to see that the real consumption possibilities of the household are unaltered — it can still purchase 10 units of C_1, 5 units of C_2, or a combination determined by their relative prices, which have not been affected by the doubling of the absolute price level. The mathematical approach to this proposition is to say that all the demand and supply functions of the economy will be homogenous of degree zero. Homogeneity of degree zero means that multiplying each of the independent variables of a function by an arbitrary constant Φ will multiply the function by Φ^0 (which is by definition equal to 1). In economic terms this means that if all prices in the economy increase by the same proportion Φ (where Φ represents a constant percentage increase) the quantities demanded and supplied will be unaffected. We can demonstrate by considering the demand and supply for commodity 1 in the model (equations 1 and 3): if each of the independent variables in the demand function is multiplied by Φ

$$C_1 = \frac{(\phi Y)}{2\phi P_1)}$$

$$= \frac{Y}{2P_1} \qquad \text{as before.}$$

Multiplying the independent variables in the supply function by the constant Φ:

$$X_1 = \frac{(\phi P_1)^3}{16(\phi w)^2(\phi r)}$$

$$= \frac{\phi^3 P_1^{\,3}}{\phi^3 16 w^2 r}$$

$$= \frac{P_1^{\,3}}{16 w^2 r} \qquad \text{as before.}$$

Multiplying all prices by Φ multiplies C_1 and X_1, the quantities demanded and supplied, by 1 (= Φ^0). In other words the quantities demanded and supplied will stand in the same relation to the relative prices in the system, no matter what the absolute level of prices.

If the absolute price level cannot be determined by the real relationships in the economy, how can the model be 'solved' in order to find the equilibrium prices? The answer is, that since what is required is a set of relative prices, we can arbitrarily set one price equal to 1 and then solve the system for all the other (relative) prices. The good with price set equal to unity is known as the 'numeraire' commodity, and the prices of all other goods are determined in terms of the numeraire. For example, suppose good 1 is the numeraire: its price will be set equal to 1. If the price of good 2 is found to be 3 when good 1 is numeraire, this means that one unit of good 2 will exchange for three units of good 1 — the price is to be interpreted in terms of the numeraire commodity.

Choosing one commodity to be the numeraire is known as the 'normalisation' procedure. If good 1 is the numeraire commodity we normalise by setting $P_1 = 1$; if good 2 is the numeraire then the normalisation involves setting $P_2 = 1$. Provided the general equilibrium system is homogeneous of degree zero it does not matter which good is chosen to be the numeraire; the same system of relative prices will emerge from the solution to the system, and the values of the 'real' variables i.e. the actual quantities demanded and supplied will be the same. This property of general equilibrium systems can be demonstrated very easily using computer programs, and we do this in Section 2.6 below.

The other aspect of general equilibrium models to be considered is known as Walras' Law. Walras' Law states that for a given set of prices, the sum of the excess demands over all markets must be equal to zero. In other words, if one market has positive excess demand, another must have excess supply; and if all but one are in balance, so is that one. More formally, Walras' Law states that in a general equilibrium model with m economic agents and n markets, if all economic agents are satisfying their budget constraints and $n-1$ markets are in equilibrium, with the quantity demanded equal to the quantity supplied, then the nth market will automatically also be in equilibrium. Alternatively, if all markets clear and all agents but one are on their budget constraints, then the last economic agent will automatically be on his budget constraint. This property of general equilibrium models, too, can be very clearly illustrated by the use of a computer program.

2.6 The Solution of the General Equilibrium System

The general equilibrium model summarised in Table 2.1 consists of 15 simultaneous equations, many of which are non-linear, and 15 unknowns. From an economic point of view the model is a very simple one: there are only two commodities, two factors of production and one consumer; there is no public sector and no foreign trade. Nevertheless, from a mathematical point of view, the solution of such a system would be difficult and tedious without a computer. Writing a computer program to solve the model not only makes it possible to solve the system of equations in a few seconds; the structure of the program shows clearly how supply and demand interact to generate equilibrium solutions in individual markets and also brings out the links between markets — in particular, the connection between the commodity markets and the factor markets. We therefore present in this section a BASIC computer program which will find a solution to the model of Table 2.1.[1]

It is assumed that readers of this book have access to a small-microcomputer. For those not yet familiar with computers the writing of simple computer programs of the kind we consider in this book need not present any difficulty. While most students today are familiar with the use of microcomputers, we include in this paragraph a few remarks for those who have not previously had experience of programming in BASIC. A computer program is a series of numbered instructions, or 'statements', written in a computer language. To write the program for the general equilibrium model requires very little programming knowledge. In order to 'translate' the equations of the model into 'BASIC' it is necessary to know the symbols for arithmetic operations

+ = add   / = divide
− = subtract   ^ = raise to the power
* = multiply

---

1. The programs in this book are written in standard BASIC and should run without difficulty on most makes of microcomputer. Some users may find minor modifications are required for their machines.

When several arithmetic operations have to be used in the same statement, brackets are used to indicate the order of operations. We illustrate by writing the statements representing the demand and supply relations for commodity 1 (equations 1 and 3 in Table 2.1).

$$C_1 = \frac{Y}{2P_1} \qquad \text{becomes} \quad \text{LET } C1 = Y/(2\star P1)$$

$$X_1 = \frac{P_1}{16w^2r} \qquad \text{becomes} \quad \text{LET } X1 = P1^\wedge 3/(16\star W \ ^\wedge 2\star R)$$

(Note that the programming language BASIC does not include the use of subscripts, nor lower case letters.) The command word LET assigns the values of the right-hand side of the equations to the variables C1 and X1. Other command words used in the program are IF . . . THEN, and GOTO whose meaning in the program will be obvious from everyday English. The INPUT statement tells the computer that a value for a variable is to be supplied by the user, and the PRINT statement causes the required information to be printed on the screen. Any statement introduced by the command word REM (short for 'remark') is ignored by the computer when running the program but can be used by the programmer to record useful information about the structure and use of the program. To write the computer program each statement in the program must be typed on a separate line, and the RETURN key pressed before entering the next line. By convention the lines of the program are numbered 10, 20, 30, . . . rather than 1, 2, 3, . . . so that additional lines can be added subsequently if required. To run the program when it is complete type RUN, and press the RETURN key. The only action subsequently required of the user is to type in initial values for variables when the computer reaches the INPUT statements.

We now have to consider how to construct a program to solve the general equilibrium model of Table 2.1 in order to find the equilibrium values of the endogenous variables. Such a model, consisting of a large number of non-linear simultaneous equations, cannot be solved by analytic means, but requires the use of an iteration procedure. An iteration procedure is one which instructs the computer to try one set of values for the variables and then, if these prove not to be the solution values, the computer is instructed to try further values until a solution is found. Such a procedure is particularly appropriate for an economic market model. A set of instructions for a single market can be given by using an IF . . . THEN statement to raise the price of the commodity in question if demand exceeds supply and an IF . . . THEN statement to lower the price of the commodity if supply exceeds demand. To bring the iteration procedure to an end it is necessary to include an instruction to stop the program when the equilibrium value(s) have been found. As demand will not normally be exactly equal to supply (because the computer works to a large number of decimal places), rather than writing the statement IF DEMAND = SUPPLY THEN GOTO (end of program), we write IF ABS (DEMAND − SUPPLY) < 0.01 THEN GOTO (end of program), where ABS means the absolute value of the expression in brackets. 0.01, 0.001, 0.0001, etc. could all be used, depending on the desired degree of accuracy.

Table 2.2 lists a BASIC computer program which will solve the general equilibrium model of Table 2.1. The program opens with two REM statements. The first summarises the main features of the model; the second is discussed below. The next two lines of the program assign values to the two exogenous variables $K^\star$ and $L^\star$ (denoted simply K and L in the computer program). Line 50 constitutes the normalisation procedure: P_1 (P1 in the computer program) is set equal to 1, and good 1 is therefore the numeraire commodity. The following three INPUT statements ask the user to supply values for P2, W and R to start off the iteration program. Any values could be supplied; we suggest P2 = 1.3, R = 0.7, and W = 0.3, and have recorded these suggestions in the second of the REM statements at the beginning of the program. (These values are suggested because they lie near the equilibrium solution; when the solution is not known, a guess must be made. The program will continue running until the equilibrium values are found. The only cost of a bad guess is the length of time taken by the iteration procedure.) Lines 90 − 190 define the supply and demand relationships and the budget constraints for the firms and the consumer in terms of the prices already supplied.

Lines 200 − 370 constitute the part of the program that solves the model using an iterative procedure. Line 200 states that if the difference between supply and demand is less than .01 in all three markets for labour, capital and good 2, the program should proceed to ('GOTO') line 380 and print out the equilibrium solutions to the model. If however supply is not (approximately) equal to demand in any of the three markets, lines 210 − 360 give

Table 2.2 Computer Program to Solve the Model of Table 2.1

```
10 REM GENERAL EQUILIBRIUM MODEL WITH ONE CONSUMER
   TWO GOODS, AND TWO FACTORS. GOOD 1 IS NUMERAIRE
20 REM SUGGESTED INPUT VALUES: P2=1.3, R=0.7, W =0.3
30 LET K = 0.8
40 LET L = 2.0
50 LET P1 = 1
60 INPUT "INITIAL VALUE FOR P2? " P2
70 INPUT "INITIAL VALUE FOR R? " R
80 INPUT "INITIAL VALUE FOR W? " W
90 LET X1 = P1^3/(16*W^2*R)
100 LET X2 = P2^3/(16*R^2*W)
110 LET K1 = ((W*X1^2)/(2*R))^(2/3)
120 LET K2 = ((2*W*X2^4)/R)^(1/3)
130 LET L1 = ((2*R*X1^4)/W)^(1/3)
140 LET L2 = ((R*X2^2)/(2*W))^(2/3)
150 LET PI1 = P1*X1-R*K1-W*L1
160 LET PI2 = P2*X2-R*K2-W*L2
170 LET Y = R*(K1+K2)+W*(L1+L2)+PI1+PI2
180 LET C1 = Y/(2*P1)
190 LET C2 = Y/(2*P2)
200 IF ABS(K-K1-K2)<0.01 AND ABS(L-L1-L2)<0.01 AND
    ABS(C2-X2)<0.01 THEN GOTO 380
210 IF (K1+K2)>K THEN PRINT "EXCESS DEMAND FOR CAPITAL"
220 IF (K1+K2)>K THEN LET R = R+.001
230 IF (K1+K2)<K THEN PRINT "EXCESS SUPPLY OF CAPITAL"
240 IF (K1+K2)<K THEN LET R = R-.001
250 PRINT "R = "R
260 IF (L1+L2)>L THEN PRINT "EXCESS DEMAND FOR LABOUR"
270 IF (L1+L2)>L THEN LET W = W+.001
280 IF (L1+L2)<L THEN PRINT "EXCESS SUPPLY OF LABOUR"
290 IF (L1+L2)<L THEN LET W = W-.001
300 PRINT "W = "W
310 IF C2>X2 THEN PRINT "EXCESS DEMAND FOR GOOD 2"
320 IF C2>X2 THEN LET P2 = P2+.001
330 IF C2<X2 THEN PRINT "EXCESS SUPPLY OF GOOD 2"
340 IF C2<X2 THEN LET P2 = P2-.001
350 PRINT "P2 = "P2
360 PRINT
370 GOTO 90
380 PRINT "EQUILIBRIUM PRICES"
390 PRINT "P1 = "P1
400 PRINT "P2 = "P2
410 PRINT "R = "R
420 PRINT "W = "W
430 PRINT
```

```
440 PRINT "EQUILIBRIUM OUTPUT AND EMPLOYMENT"
450 PRINT "X1 = "X1
460 PRINT "X2 = "X2
470 PRINT "K1 = "K1
480 PRINT "K2 = "K2
490 PRINT "L1 = "L1
500 PRINT "L2 = "L2
510 PRINT
520 PRINT "CHECK WALRAS' LAW"
530 PRINT "C1 = "C1, " X1 = "X1
```

instructions to raise the relevant price if demand exceeds supply and to lower the relevant price if supply exceeds demand; the program then returns to line 90 (instructed by line 370) and recalculates all the values using the new prices.

When supply is approximately equal to demand in the three markets for good 2, capital and labour, lines 380 – 530 cause the computer to print the equilibrium solutions for the variables of the model on the screen. The lines 520 and 530 of the program are of particular interest. It was noted above that Walras' Law states that if n-1 of the equations of a general equilibrium model are satisfied, the nth equation will also be satisfied. The iteration procedure used in the above program ensured that excess demand and excess supply are eliminated in the markets for good 2, labour and capital, and lines 150 – 170 ensure that the budget constraints are all satisfied. Nothing was said about the market for good 1, so at the end of the program we print out the solution values for the demand for good 1 and the supply of good 1. By Walras' Law, excess demand in this remaining market should be equal to zero, so if the program has run correctly, the values of C1 and X1 should be approximately equal; if not there is something wrong with either the model or the computer program. Printing out the supply and demand relations for the omitted market not only illustrates Walras' Law but also constitutes a valuable check on the general equilibrium program. We therefore include a statement checking the operation of Walras' Law at the end of the programs in this book.

The student who wishes to try out the above program should find the following equilibrium values for the variables:[1]

---

1. As the program is designed to find solutions within 0.01 of the true equilibrium values, individual solutions may differ by up to 0.01 from the values given here, but they should not differ by more than 0.01.

P1 = 1   P2 = 1.25   R = 0.77   W = 0.31
X1 = 0.83   X2 = 0.66
K1 = 0.27   K2 = 0.53   L1 = 1.34   L2 = 0.66

Once the computer program has been written it can be used to perform interesting 'experiments'. For example, it is possible to examine the effects on the general equilibrium system of increasing one of the initial factor endowments of the economy. Either factor could be increased or decreased: one experiment would be to let the capital stock increase from 0.8 to 1.0 by re-writing line 30 of the program of Table 2.2 to read

30 LET K = 1.0

and to compare the results from running this program with the solution values given above. The student could then consider what economic explanations can be given for the changes in the relative prices and the changes in the quantities of the two goods supplied. A further experiment would be to use the original quantity for the initial endowment of capital and to alter line 40 of the program to model the consequences of increasing the initial endowment of labour. The results of this program could then be compared with the solutions to the two earlier programs.

We conclude this section by presenting a different computer program written to solve the model of Table 2.1, using good 2 as numeraire. In the program of Table 2.3, P2 is set equal to 1 and the student should compare Table 2.3 carefully with Table 2.2 noting the necessary changes in the program. When this program is RUN, the equilibrium solutions are seen to be

P1 = 0.80   P2 = 1   R = 0.62   W = 0.25
X1 = 0.83   X2 = 0.66
K1 = 0.27   K2 = 0.53   L1 = 1.34   L2 = 0.66

If these solutions are compared with those resulting from the program of Table 2.2, it will be seen that the change of numeraire leads to different absolute prices, but does not change the relative prices of the system. For example, the ratio P1/P2 is equal to 0.8 in both sets of solutions, and the reader can check that the other relative prices are unaffected by the change of numeraire. The values of the real variables of the model, those giving the values of output and employment, are seen to be the same in both cases.

Table 2.3 Computer Program to Solve the Model of Table 2.1 with Good 2 as Numeraire

```
10 REM GENERAL EQUILIBRIUM MODEL WITH ONE CONSUMER,
   TWO GOODS AND TWO FACTORS. GOOD 2 IS NUMERAIRE.
20 REM SUGGESTED INPUT VALUES: P1=0.8, R=0.6, W = 0.25
30 LET K = 0.8
40 LET L = 2.0
50 LET P2 = 1
60 INPUT "INITIAL VALUE FOR P1? " P1
70 INPUT "INITIAL VALUE FOR R?  " R
80 INPUT "INITIAL VALUE FOR W?  " W
90 LET X1 = P1^3/(16*W^2*R)
100 LET X2 = P2^3/(16*R^2*W)
110 LET K1 = ((W*X1^2)/(2*R))^(2/3)
120 LET K2 = ((2*W*X2^4)/R)^(1/3)
130 LET L1 = ((2*R*X1^4)/W)^(1/3)
140 LET L2 = ((R*X2^2)/(2*W))^(2/3)
150 LET PI1 = P1*X1-R*K1-W*L1
160 LET PI2 = P2*X2-R*K2-W*L2
170 LET Y = R*(K1+K2)+W*(L1+L2)+PI1+PI2
180 LET C1 = Y/(2*P1)
190 LET C2 = Y/(2*P2)
200 IF ABS(K-K1-K2)<0.01 AND ABS(L-L1-L2)<0.01 AND
    ABS(C1-X1)<0.01 THEN GOTO 380
210 IF (K1+K2)>K THEN PRINT "EXCESS DEMAND FOR CAPITAL"
220 IF (K1+K2)>K THEN LET R = R+.001
230 IF (K1+K2)<K THEN PRINT "EXCESS SUPPLY OF CAPITAL"
240 IF (K1+K2)<K THEN LET R = R-.001
250 PRINT "R = "R
260 IF (L1+L2)>L THEN PRINT "EXCESS DEMAND FOR LABOUR"
270 IF (L1+L2)>L THEN LET W = W+.001
280 IF (L1+L2)<L THEN PRINT "EXCESS SUPPLY OF LABOUR"
290 IF (L1+L2)<L THEN LET W = W-.001
300 PRINT "W = "W
310 IF C1>X1 THEN PRINT "EXCESS DEMAND FOR GOOD 1"
320 IF C1>X1 THEN LET P1 = P1+.001
330 IF C1<X1 THEN PRINT "EXCESS SUPPLY OF GOOD 1"
340 IF C1<X1 THEN LET P1 = P1-.001
350 PRINT "P1= "P1
360 PRINT
370 GOTO 90
380 PRINT "EQUILIBRIUM PRICES"
390 PRINT "P1 = "P1
400 PRINT "P2 = "P2
410 PRINT "R = "R
420 PRINT "W = "W
```

```
430 PRINT
440 PRINT "EQUILIBRIUM OUTPUT AND EMPLOYMENT"
450 PRINT "X1 = "X1
460 PRINT "X2 = "X2
470 PRINT "K1 = "K1
480 PRINT "K2 = "K2
490 PRINT "L1 = "L1
500 PRINT "L2 = "L2
510 PRINT
520 PRINT "CHECK WALRAS' LAW"
530 PRINT "C2 = "C2, " X2 = "X2
```

APPENDIX

The Mathematics of Constrained Optimisation

Constrained optimisation is a branch of the differential calculus. For a full introduction to the solution of constrained optimisation problems using the method of Lagrange multipliers the reader is referred to any of the texts recommended in the 'Suggestions for Further Reading' at the end of the book. The following paragraphs simply present a summary of the procedure used in the derivation of demand and supply functions in Chapter 2.

A constrained optimisation problem involves specifying what is to be optimised (the objective function) and the nature of the constraints. The objective function is known as the maximand if the problem is one of maximisation and as the minimand if the problem is one of minimisation. The use of Lagrange multipliers, introduced below, transforms the constrained optimisation problem into one which can be handled by the familiar methods of unconstrained optimisation. We assume that the objective function is a function of n variables and has the general form

$$F(x_1, x_2, \ldots x_n) \tag{A.1}$$

Any number of constraints can be incorporated in the problem, but to simplify the presentation we assume that there is only one constraint of the form

$$G(x_1, x_2, \ldots x_n) = B \tag{A.2}$$

This formulation of the constraint tells us that the constraint is also a function of the same n variables as the objective function and that the value of the function must be exactly equal to B.[1]

Before the constraint can be used in the problem it has to be rewritten in the implicit form

$$G(x_1, x_2, \ldots x_n) - B = 0 \tag{A.2a}$$

To use the Lagrange multiplier method a new Lagrangean expression is formed:

---

1. In classical optimisation problems of the kind discussed here, the constraint relation must be exactly satisfied. Problems where the constraint takes the form
$$G(x_1, x_2, \ldots x_n) < \text{ or } > B$$
are handled by different mathematical procedures using linear or non-linear programming methods.

$$Z = F(x_1, x_2, \ldots x_n) + \lambda[G(x_1, x_2, \ldots x_n) - B] \qquad (A.3)$$

It will be seen that the Lagrangean consists of two parts. The first term on the right-hand side of the equation is the objective function. The second term consists of the constraint in implicit form (A.2a) multiplied by λ, the undetermined Lagrange multiplier. The purpose of including the multiplier λ is explained below. To examine the Lagrangean expression for maximum or minimum values we proceed as usual by setting the first-order partial derivatives equal to zero. This gives the necessary conditions for an optimum value. The Lagrangean can be differentiated with respect to each of the n independent variables and with respect to λ, so there will be $n+1$ partial derivatives to be considered. These partial derivatives are

$$\delta Z/\delta x_1 = \delta F/\delta x_1 + \lambda \delta G/\delta x_1$$
$$\delta Z/\delta x_2 = \delta F/\delta x_2 + \lambda \delta G/\delta x_2$$
$$\text{-----------------------}$$
$$\delta Z/\delta x_n = \delta F/\delta x_n + \lambda \delta G/\delta x_n$$
$$\delta Z/\delta \lambda = G(x_1, x_2, \ldots x_n) - B$$

Setting each of these partial derivatives equal to zero yields the following $n+1$ equations:

$$\delta F/\delta x_1 + \lambda \delta G/\delta x_1 = 0$$
$$\delta F/\delta x_2 + \lambda \delta G/\delta x_2 = 0$$
$$\text{--------------------} \qquad (A.4)$$
$$\delta F/\delta x_n + \lambda \delta G/\delta x_n = 0$$
$$G(x_1, x_2, \ldots x_n) - B = 0$$

It will be immediately obvious that the presence of the last equation in the equation set (A.4) ensures that the constraint (A.2) is exactly satisfied. That is the purpose of the undetermined Lagrange multiplier; it builds the constraint into the solution of the optimisation problem because the condition $\delta Z/\delta \lambda = 0$ guarantees that the constraint will be exactly fulfilled.

Second-order conditions for constrained optimisation problems, needed to distinguish between constrained maxima and constrained minima, are complex. They turn upon the signs of the second-order partial derivatives and can be found in, for instance, Chiang (1984). However, there is no need to worry about the second-order conditions if the objective function is known to be concave or quasi-concave at all points in its domain (in which case satisfaction of the first-order conditions will be sufficient to establish a maximum) or convex or quasi-convex at all points (in which case satisfaction of the first order conditions will establish a minimum). In the text we assume appropriate forms for the utility functions and production functions that satisfy these conditions.

A Numerical Example

Find the values of x and y that maximise the function $F(x,y) = 10x^{1/2}y^{1/2}$ subject to the constraint $5x + 2y = 200$. (Take second-order conditions for granted.)

Rewriting the constraint in implicit form $5x + 2y - 200 = 0$, form the Lagrangean

$$Z = 10x^{1/2}y^{1/2} + \lambda(5x + 2y - 200)$$

and set the partial derivatives $\delta Z/\delta x = \delta Z/\delta y = \delta Z/\delta \lambda = 0$ to give the following three equations

$$\frac{\delta Z}{\delta x} = \frac{5y^{1/2}}{x^{1/2}} + 5\lambda = 0 \tag{A.5}$$

$$\frac{\delta Z}{\delta y} = \frac{5x^{1/2}}{y^{1/2}} + 2\lambda = 0 \tag{A.6}$$

$$\frac{\delta Z}{\delta \lambda} = 5x + 2y - 200 = 0 \tag{A.7}$$

Solving equations (A.5) and (A.6) for λ and equating the resulting expressions gives the equation

$$5x = 2y \tag{A.8}$$

By solving the pair of simultaneous equations in x and y, (A.7) and (A.8), the values of x and y that maximise the objective function subject to the constraint are seen to be

$$x = 20 \qquad y = 50.$$

References

Chiang, A. (1984) *Fundamental Methods of Mathematical Economics* (3rd edn), McGraw-Hill.

Deaton, A. and Muellbauer, J. (1980) *Economics and Consumer Behaviour*, Cambridge University Press.

Hebden, J. (1983) *Applications of Econometrics*, Philip Allan.

3
CONSTANT RETURNS TO SCALE: AN ALTERNATIVE MODEL

3.1 Introduction

The analysis of Chapters 1 and 2 was based on a model of market behaviour which assumed that in each market prices would adjust until an equilibrium was established in which the demand price of the consumer was equal to the supply price of the producer. This approach to general equilibrium analysis was characteristic of the early development of the subject but, as noted by Arrow (1974), there was a difficulty: 'The assumptions on production were not the same as those used in the analysis of production itself. In the latter, a common, though not universal assumption was that of constant returns to scale'. With constant returns to scale, profit-maximising behaviour on the part of producers no longer leads to a unique relation between the quantity of a good supplied and its price. The reason for this is that if an activity is profitable at one level of output at existing prices, then for example doubling output will double profits, and there will in general be a large and indeterminate number of output levels compatible with a given set of relative prices. (Conversely, if at the given set of prices production is not profitable at the existing level of output, it will not be profitable at any other output level.) With constant returns to scale, it is no longer possible to derive a supply function for the profit-maximising firm which relates particular levels of output to the price of the product. This raises the question of how market equilibrium is to be established in general equilibrium models which assume constant returns to scale.

In this chapter we discuss the implications of constant returns to scale production functions for the two-sector general equilibrium model, and in the next chapter we use a numerical example to show how a general equilibrium model with constant returns to scale can be solved. Section 3.2 uses the Cobb-Douglas production function with constant returns to scale to illustrate the fact that with a linearly homogenous production function it is possible to derive factor demand functions and unit cost equations, but not supply functions. Section 3.3 sets up a formal model for an economy with constant returns to scale in production, and Section 3.4 extends the analysis by showing how inter-industry flows can be included in the model. The analysis of this chapter and the numerical examples of Chapter 4 pave the way for the discussion in Chapter 5 of the international trade theory model which is based on the assumption of constant returns to scale in production.

3.2 The Cobb–Douglas Production Function with Constant Returns to Scale

The general form of the Cobb–Douglas production function is

$$X_i = K_i^\alpha L_i^\beta \tag{3.1}$$

and specific examples of this functional form were used for the firms' production functions in the numerical example of Chapter 2. The Cobb–Douglas function has the mathematical property of being homogenous of degree $\alpha + \beta$. It is easy to show, using the method of the previous chapter, that multiplying both K_i and L_i by a constant Φ, multiplies the function by $\Phi^{\alpha+\beta}$:

$$
\begin{aligned}
(\Phi K_i)^\alpha (\Phi L_i)^\beta \\
= \quad \Phi^{\alpha+\beta} K_i^\alpha L_i^\beta \\
= \quad \Phi^{\alpha+\beta} X_i
\end{aligned}
$$

The economic interpretation of this property of the Cobb–Douglas production function is that the function can exhibit varying returns to scale, depending upon the values taken by α and β. If $\alpha+\beta > 1$, there are increasing returns to scale, and increasing the inputs of capital and labour by a given proportion will lead output to increase by a greater proportion; if $\alpha + \beta < 1$, there are decreasing returns to scale, and a given proportionate increase in factor inputs will lead to a smaller proportionate increase in output; if $\alpha + \beta = 1$, there are constant returns to scale. In this case the function is said to be linearly homogenous, and can be represented by

$$X_i = K_i^\alpha L_i^{1-\alpha} \tag{3.2}$$

With all linearly homogenous production functions, increasing all the factor inputs by a given proportion will lead to an equi-proportionate increase in output.

The Cobb–Douglas functions used to derive supply functions for the two firms in the numerical example of Chapter 2 exhibited decreasing returns to scale. In this section we use the linearly homogenous version of the Cobb–Douglas function (3.2) to consider the implications of constant returns to scale for a profit-maximising firm.

The following analysis proceeds along the same lines as that of Section 2.3 in the previous chapter. It will be recalled that the first stage in the analysis of the firm's optimising behaviour consists of establishing the minimum cost for any level of production, given the nature of the production function and the prices of the factors of production. Using r and w as before to represent respectively the prices of capital and labour the total cost of the ith firm (TC_i) is given by

$$TC_i = rK_i + wL_i \tag{3.3}$$

From (3.2) we can solve for K_i in terms of X_i and L_i:

$$K_i = \left(\frac{X_i}{L_i^{1-\alpha}} \right)^{\frac{1}{\alpha}} \tag{3.4}$$

and substituting (3.4) in (3.3) gives

$$TC_i = r \left(\frac{X_i}{L_i^{1-\alpha}} \right)^{\frac{1}{\alpha}} + wL_i \tag{3.5}$$

Minimising this function with respect to L_i gives the necessary condition

$$\frac{\delta TC_i}{\delta L_i} = -r \left(\frac{1-\alpha}{\alpha} \right) \left(\frac{X_i}{L_i} \right)^{\frac{1}{\alpha}} + w = 0 \tag{3.6}$$

and solving for L_i to find the conditional demand for labour:

$$L_i = \left(\frac{1-\alpha}{\alpha} \frac{r}{w} \right)^{\alpha} X_i \tag{3.7}$$

Similarly, substituting for L_i from (3.2) in (3.3) gives

$$TC_i = rK_i + w \left(\frac{X_i}{K_i^{\alpha}} \right)^{\frac{1}{1-\alpha}} \tag{3.8}$$

and setting $\dfrac{\delta TC_i}{\delta K_i} = 0$

$$\frac{\delta TC_i}{\delta K_i} = r - w \left(\frac{\alpha}{1-\alpha}\right)\left(\frac{X_i}{K_i}\right)^{\frac{1}{1-\alpha}} = 0 \tag{3.9}$$

enables us to derive the conditional demand for capital:

$$K_i = \left(\frac{\alpha}{1-\alpha}\,\frac{w}{r}\right)^{1-\alpha} X_i \tag{3.10}$$

The two equations (3.7) and (3.10) represent the two conditional demands for the factors of production labour and capital when the firm's production function is given by the constant returns to scale version of the Cobb-Douglas function represented by equation (3.2).

In the case of the firm with a decreasing returns to scale production function the next stage is, as discussed in the context of the numerical example of the preceeding chapter, to find the firm's profit-maximising level of output. Profits are measured by the difference between total revenue and total cost at different levels of output, and with decreasing returns to scale the optimum level of output can be determined by finding the value of output X_i that maximises the value of profits. If we attempt to follow this procedure for the firm with the constant returns to scale technology we derive the following results. Representing the product price by P_i and profits by Π_i

$$\Pi_i = P_i X_i - rK_i - wL_i \tag{3.11}$$

and substituting the conditional demands for capital and labour derived above

$$\Pi_i = P_i X_i - r\left[\left(\frac{\alpha}{1-\alpha}\,\frac{w}{r}\right)^{1-\alpha} X_i\right] - w\left[\left(\frac{1-\alpha}{\alpha}\,\frac{r}{w}\right)^{\alpha} X_i\right] \tag{3.12}$$

It is not possible to find the profit-maximising level of output X_i by setting the following derivative of (3.12) equal to zero:

$$\frac{\delta\Pi}{\delta X_i} = P_i - r\left(\frac{\alpha}{1-\alpha}\,\frac{w}{r}\right)^{1-\alpha} - w\left(\frac{1-\alpha}{\alpha}\,\frac{r}{w}\right)^{\alpha} \tag{3.13}$$

as this expression does not contain the term X_1 on the right hand side, showing that the rate of change of profit with respect to changes in output is not a function of the level of output but only of the prices P_i, w and r. Equating the partial derivative $\delta\Pi/\delta X_1$ to zero does not enable us to solve for a profit-maximising level of output, but yields the 'unit price' or 'unit cost' equation for the firm:

$$P_i = r\left(\frac{\alpha}{1-\alpha}\frac{w}{r}\right)^{1-\alpha} + w\left(\frac{1-\alpha}{\alpha}\frac{r}{w}\right)^{\alpha} \tag{3.14}$$

The reason why this equation is called the unit cost equation is more clearly seen by returning to the equations for the conditional factor demands for capital and labour (equations 3.7 and 3.10). These two equations can be re-written in terms of factor demand per unit of output by dividing both sides of the equations by X_i. Denoting the per unit factor demands for capital and labour by the lower case letters k_i and l_i we have

$$k_i = \frac{K_i}{X_i} = \left(\frac{\alpha}{1-\alpha}\frac{w}{r}\right)^{1-\alpha} \tag{3.15}$$

$$l_i = \frac{L_i}{X_i} = \left(\frac{1-\alpha}{\alpha}\frac{r}{w}\right)^{\alpha} \tag{3.16}$$

showing that the per unit factor demands are functions of the two factor prices r and w. By using (3.15) and (3.16) the expression defining the firm's profits (equation 3.12) can be written in terms of k_i and l_i

$$\Pi = P_i X_i - r k_i X_i - w l_i X_i \tag{3.17}$$

and the unit cost equation (3.14) (originally derived by setting $\delta\Pi/\delta X_i = 0$) can also be written in terms of k_i and l_i:

$$P_i = r k_i + w l_i \tag{3.18}$$

Both the left-hand side and the right-hand side of the equation are now seen to be in per unit terms. P_i is the price per unit of X_i; k_i and l_i represent the quantities of the two factors demanded per unit of X_i produced, so the right-hand side of equation (3.18) measures the cost per unit of X_i. This expression demonstrates the proposition, familiar from elementary economic theory, that profit-maximisation leads marginal revenue to be equated to the marginal cost of production which, with constant returns to scale, is also the average cost of production.

The unit price, or unit cost, equation also makes it clear that the perfectly competitive profit-maximising firm with constant returns to scale will make zero profits. (Multiplying both sides of (3.18) by X_i will show that the firm's total revenue is equal to its total costs.) This conclusion can be related to the analysis in the Introduction to this chapter which pointed out that any firm with constant returns making positive profits would be constantly expanding, while any firm making a loss at the prevailing set of relative prices would be forced to close down. Only with zero profits can a firm with a constant returns to scale technology be in equilibrium, and this equilibrium is compatible with any one of the set of possible output levels.

The previous analysis used a Cobb-Douglas function to demonstrate that there is no supply function with a constant returns to scale production function. This analysis could be repeated for other linearly homogenous production functions, for example the widely used CES (constant elasticity of substitution) function which has the form

$$X = (aK^{-\beta} + bL^{-\beta})^{-1/\beta} \qquad (3.19)$$

where, as before, X measures output, K, capital, and L, labour. With this function, too, conditional factor demand functions can be derived from a cost minimisation exercise, and unit cost relations can be established. The two-sector model presented in the following section does not depend upon the firms' production functions taking any specific form, but it does assume constant returns to scale in the production of both commodities. In the numerical example of Chapter 4, we draw upon the algebraic analysis of this section to illustrate the constant returns to scale model using Cobb-Douglas production functions.

3.3 The Equations of the Model

In Chapter 1 we showed that with two goods, two factors, and one consumer, a general equilibrium system could be defined by a set of 15 equations with 15 endogenous variables. In that chapter it was implicitly assumed that production was characterised by decreasing returns to scale so that each firm could be assumed to have a supply function, and each firm could be expected to make profits equal to the difference between its revenue from the sale of its product, and its costs of production. In this section we consider what changes to the model will be required if constant returns to scale are assumed in the economy.

We retain the assumption that the consumer maximises his utility subject to the product prices and the level of his income, so the market demand equations [(1.1) and (1.2) in Chapter 1] are unchanged. As explained above, there are no supply functions with constant returns to scale so equations (1.3) and (1.4) have to be replaced by the unit price equations for each firm:

$$P_1 = rk_1 + wl_1 \tag{3.20}$$
$$P_2 = rk_2 + wl_2 \tag{3.21}$$

These unit price equations have been defined in terms of the per unit factor requirements k_i and l_i, so equations defining these variables have to be added to the model. As demonstrated above, in the example of the Cobb–Douglas production function, the per unit factor demand functions are a function of the factor prices, w and r. We have therefore:

$$k_i = k_i(w,r) \qquad i = 1,2 \tag{3.22}$$
$$l_i = l_i(w,r) \qquad i = 1,2 \tag{3.23}$$

where

$$k_i = \frac{K_i}{X_i} \quad i = 1,2 \tag{3.24}$$

$$l_i = \frac{L_i}{X_i} \quad i = 1,2 \tag{3.25}$$

The assumption of constant returns to scale has meant that four new variables, k_1, k_2, l_1 and l_2 have been introduced into the model. Two variables that appear in the decreasing returns to scale model are, however, absent from the model of this chapter. As noted at the end of the previous section, any general equilibrium solution for a model assuming constant returns to scale implies zero profits for the private sector producers. The variables Π_1 and Π_2 can therefore be dropped, and will not appear either in equations defining the income of the firms or in the equation defining the income of the consumer. No further alterations to the model of Chapter 1 are required and we set out in Table 3.1 the full general equilibrium model for the constant returns to scale economy.

A specific version of this general constant returns to scale model

Table 3.1 Model of a Two-sector Economy with Constant Returns to Scale

---

COMMODITY MARKETS

Demand

$$C_1 = C_1(P_1, P_2, Y) \tag{1}$$
$$C_2 = C_2(P_1, P_2, Y) \tag{2}$$

Unit price
  equations

$$P_1 = rk_1 + wl_1 \tag{3}$$
$$P_2 = rk_2 + wl_2 \tag{4}$$

Market clearing

$$C_1 = X_1 \tag{5}$$
$$C_2 = X_2 \tag{6}$$

FACTOR MARKETS

Demand

$$k_1 = k_1(w, r) \tag{7}$$
$$K_1 = k_1 X_1 \tag{8}$$
$$k_2 = k_2(w, r) \tag{9}$$
$$K_2 = k_2 X_2 \tag{10}$$
$$l_1 = l_1(w, r) \tag{11}$$
$$L_1 = l_1 X_1 \tag{12}$$
$$l_2 = l_2(w, r) \tag{13}$$
$$L_2 = l_2 X_2 \tag{14}$$

Market clearing

$$K_1 + K_2 = K^\star \tag{15}$$
$$L_1 + L_2 = L^\star \tag{16}$$

CONSUMER'S INCOME

$$Y = r(K_1 + K_2) + w(L_1 + L_2) \tag{17}$$

The 17 endogenous variables are C_1 C_2 X_1 X_2 K_1 K_2 L_1 L_2
k_1 k_2 l_1 l_2 P_1 P_2 w r Y
The variables $K^\star$ and $L^\star$ are exogenous.

---

is formulated and solved in the next chapter. Before proceeding to the numerical example, however, we discuss a more comprehensive version of the constant returns to scale model which incorporates intermediate inputs in the production functions of the firms.

3.4   The Model with Inter-Industry Flows

The supply side of the economy in the models presented so far has been based upon production functions of the general form $X_i = X_i(K_i, L_i)$. These are of course highly stylised versions of the relations of production in the real world, and one obvious step towards greater realism is to incorporate material inputs into the production functions. In a closed economy these material inputs must consist of part of the output from the producing sectors. If we return to the circular flow diagram it will be necessary to add inter-industry flows to the diagram to represent these intermediate inputs:

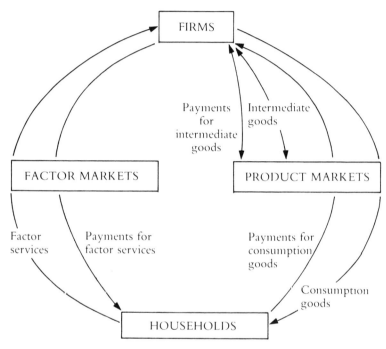

Figure 3.1 The Circular Flow Diagram with Intermediate Goods Included

Figure 3.1 shows that the output of each industry will go partly as before to satisfy final demand, and partly to become intermediate inputs in the production process. When modelling the supply side of the economy illustrated in the circular flow diagram of Figure 3.1, the production functions will include as inputs not only the primary factors of production, but also the intermediate goods supplied by the industrial sector.

The structure of an economy including intermediate goods can be represented by a system of input-output accounts, originally devised by W. Leontief and widely used in planning exercises. In developing an input-output version of the two-sector model we make the strong assumption, usual in the Leontief system, that inter-mediate inputs are required in fixed proportion to output in each industry. Thus if the amount of good i used as an intermediate input in the production of good j is represented by x_{ij}, the ratio x_{ij}/X_j is assumed to be a constant, represented by the input-output coefficient a_{ij}:

$$\frac{x_{ij}}{X_j} = a_{ij} \tag{3.26}$$

The total production of each good must be enough to satisfy both the final and the intermediate demands. Using C_i to represent the final demand for the output of firm i by the consumer, and the expression implied by (3.26) for the inter-industry flows x_{ij}, the relations in the two-sector closed economy are summarised in Table 3.2:

Table 3.2 Two-sector Economy with Inter-Industry Flows

	Inputs to industry 1	Input to industry 2	Final consumption	Total output
Industry 1	$a_{11}X_1$	$a_{12}X_2$	C_1	X_1
Industry 2	$a_{21}X_1$	$a_{22}X_2$	C_2	X_2
Capital	K_1	K_2		$K^\star$
Labour	L_1	L_2		$L^\star$

Total output of the two firms is given by:

$$X_1 = a_{11}X_1 + a_{12}X_2 + C_1 \tag{3.27}$$
$$X_2 = a_{21}X_1 + a_{22}X_2 + C_2 \tag{3.28}$$

Equations (3.27) and (3.28) are known as the material balance equations in the input-output version of the two-sector model. (If the coefficients a_{11} and a_{22} are not equal to zero, the industry in question uses part of its output as an input — for example, machines in a machine-tool industry, or seed-corn in farming.) It will be apparent that determining the equilibrium output of X_i in an input-output system requires the simultaneous solution of all the material balance equations. This solution can be expressed most compactly using matrix notation: defining

$$\mathbf{X} = \begin{bmatrix} X_1 \\ X_2 \end{bmatrix} \quad \mathbf{A} = \begin{bmatrix} a_{11} & a_{12} \\ a_{21} & a_{22} \end{bmatrix} \quad \mathbf{C} = \begin{bmatrix} C_1 \\ C_2 \end{bmatrix}$$

the system of equations (3.27) and (3.28) can be represented by

$$X = AX + C \qquad (3.29)$$

with the solution

$$X = (I - A)^{-1}C \qquad (3.30)$$

where I is the identity matrix.

What form does the production function take in this version of the model? The assumption of fixed coefficients for the intermediate inputs implies that there is no substitution possible between these inputs. The value-added component of the production function can be modelled either by making the same assumption for the primary inputs and assuming a fixed labour coefficient and a fixed capital coefficient, or by assuming that substitution between the primary factors is possible within the value-added component of the production function. In either case, if the relation

$$V_j = V_j(K_j, L_j) \qquad (3.31)$$

is used to represent the value-added component in the production function for firm j, the production function can be represented by

$$X_j = X_j(x_{ij}, V_j) \qquad i = 1,2 \qquad (3.32)$$

where x_{ij} is defined by means of (3.26). A useful convention is to define one unit of value added, V_j, as that quantity of value-added required to produce one unit of output X_j; (3.32) can then be written directly as

$$X_j = X_j (x_{ij}, K_j, L_j) \qquad (3.33)$$

In order to preserve the full-employment assumption of our two-sector model, we shall assume that substitution between the primary factors K and L is possible, and that (3.31) represents a linearly homogenous function such as the Cobb-Douglas or the CES functions discussed earlier. The derivation of the conditional factor demand functions then proceeds on exactly the same lines as before with the per unit factor demands being functions of the factor prices r and w. With these assumptions the production functions (3.33) exhibit constant returns to scale, and profit-maximising behaviour on the part of producers will again mean that price per unit of output will be equated with the unit cost of production. In the input-output model, however, cost per unit will include not only capital and labour costs, but also the cost per unit of inter-industry purchases. The total cost of intermediate inputs in industry j purchased from industry i will be given by

$$P_i x_{ij} = P_i a_{ij} X_j \qquad (3.34)$$

(from (3.26)) and the cost per unit of industry j's inputs will be the total cost of the input divided by X_j, which from (3.34) is $a_{ij} P_i$. The unit price equations for the two firms are therefore

$$P_1 = a_{11} P_1 + a_{21} P_2 + r k_1 + w l_1 \qquad (3.35)$$
$$P_2 = a_{12} P_1 + a_{22} P_2 + r k_2 + w l_2 \qquad (3.36)$$

where k_i and l_i are as before the per unit requirements of capital and labour.

The two-sector general equilibrium model incorporating intermediate inputs in production can be described by the model of Table 3.1 with four changes. The unit price equations [equations (3) and (4) in Table 3.1] will be replaced by (3.35) and (3.36), and the market clearing equations [equations (5) and (6) in Table 3.1] will be replaced by the commodity balance equations (3.27) and (3.28). No new variables have entered the system which consists as before of seventeen equations in seventeen endogenous variables. The input-output technology has implications for the methodology employed in solving the model which will be discussed in the context of the numerical example in the next chapter, but the fundamental nature of the general equilibrium system is unaltered by this extension of the model. In the remaining chapters of the book we revert, for simplicity, to models with only primary factors represented in the production functions; but the analysis of this chapter and the next make it possible for any interested reader to extend the subsequent models to include inter-industry flows on the production side of the economy.

References

Arrow, K.J. (1974) 'General economic equilibrium: purpose, analytic techniques, collective choice', *American Economic Review*, Vol. 64, pp. 253–72.

4

CONSTANT RETURNS TO SCALE: NUMERICAL EXAMPLES

4.1 Introduction

The last chapter considered two versions of the constant returns to scale model. In the first version, the production functions incorporated only primary inputs; in the second version, inter-mediate inputs were also considered, by means of an input–output approach to the modelling of the supply side of the economy. This chapter provides a specific example of each of these two models, together with suggested computer programs for finding the general equilibrium solution for each. For the first example we draw upon the analysis of Section 3.2 and use Cobb–Douglas production functions for each of the two firms in the two-good economy. The second example retains these functional relationships for the primary inputs, and shows how the specification of the model and the procedure for solving the general equilibrium system are affected by the inclusion of inter-industry flows. As noted in the Introduction to the last chapter, international trade theory makes extensive use of two-sector models which assume constant returns to scale, and the examples of this chapter will provide the basis for the open economy model of the next chapter.

4.2 A Model with Cobb–Douglas Production Functions

The version of the two-sector model presented in this section is an adaptation of that introduced in Chapter 2. As in the earlier model, we assume a single consumer, two goods, and two factors of production. The same utility function is assumed for the consumer:

$$U = C_1^{1/2}C_2^{1/2} \tag{4.1}$$

giving rise to the same demand functions

$$C_1 = \frac{Y}{2P_1} \tag{4.2}$$

$$C_2 = \frac{Y}{2P_2} \tag{4.3}$$

where, as before, C_i is the quantity demanded of the ith good; P_i is its price, and Y is the consumer's income defined in this model by

$$Y = r(K_1 + K_2) + w(L_1 + L_2) \tag{4.4}$$

where K_i and L_i represent respectively employment of capital and labour by the ith firm, and r and w represent the two factor prices. It will be noted that, as explained in the previous chapter, no profits are earned with constant returns to scale so this variable is absent from the equation describing the consumer's income in this version of the model.

On the supply side of the economy we assume that the two production functions can be represented by Cobb-Douglas production functions with the following parameters:

$$X_1 = K_1^{1/4}L_1^{3/4} \tag{4.5}$$
$$X_2 = K_2^{1/2}L_2^{1/2} \tag{4.6}$$

It will be seen that in both functions the exponents on the factor inputs sum to 1, thus guaranteeing constant returns to scale in production.

The procedure for deriving conditional factor demand functions and unit price equations using Cobb-Douglas production functions was explained at length in Section 3.2 of the previous chapter. We do not go over the same ground again for each of the above, but present the resulting equations which will be incorporated in our numerical example, and leave the detailed mathematics as an exercise for the interested student.

The conditional factor demand functions for firm 1 are given by

$$K_1 = X_1 \left(\frac{w}{3r} \right)^{\frac{3}{4}} \tag{4.7}$$

$$L_1 = X_1 \left(\frac{3r}{w} \right)^{\frac{1}{4}} \tag{4.8}$$

or, in per unit form

$$k_1 = \frac{K_1}{X_1} = \left(\frac{w}{3r}\right)^{\frac{3}{4}} \tag{4.9}$$

$$l_1 = \frac{L_1}{X_1} = \left(\frac{3r}{w}\right)^{\frac{1}{4}} \tag{4.10}$$

and the unit price equation for firm 1 is given by

$$P_1 = rk_1 + wl_1 \tag{4.11}$$

The corresponding functions for firm 2 are given by

$$K_2 = X_2\left(\frac{w}{r}\right)^{\frac{1}{2}} \tag{4.12}$$

$$L_2 = X_2\left(\frac{r}{w}\right)^{\frac{1}{2}} \tag{4.13}$$

$$k_2 = \frac{K_2}{X_2} = \left(\frac{w}{r}\right)^{\frac{1}{2}} \tag{4.14}$$

$$l_2 = \frac{L_2}{X_2} = \left(\frac{r}{w}\right)^{\frac{1}{2}} \tag{4.15}$$

$$P_2 = rk_2 + wl_2 \tag{4.16}$$

The full general equilibrium model for our specific numerical example is presented in Table 4.1 which is based on Table 3.2 of the previous chapter, but incorporates the specific demand and supply functions derived above from the consumer's utility function (4.1) and the firms' production functions (4.5) and (4.6).

In the numerical example of Chapter 2, where decreasing returns to scale were assumed, the equilibrium prices in each of the commodity markets and in each factor market were independently determined by the forces of supply and demand. In the constant returns to scale model of this chapter, where there are no supply functions in the commodity markets, the prices of the two commodities are determined by their costs of production, which in turn depend upon the factor prices r and w. This can be seen from the unit price equations (3) and (4) in Table 4.1; once r and w have been determined, P_1 and P_2 are also determined. This implies a

Table 4.1 A Model with Constant Returns to Scale

COMMODITY MARKETS

Demand

$$C_1 = \frac{Y}{2P_1} \tag{1}$$

$$C_2 = \frac{Y}{2P_2} \tag{2}$$

Unit price $P_1 = rk_1 + wl_1$ (3)
equations $P_2 = rk_2 + wl_2$ (4)

Market clearing $C_1 = X_1$ (5)
                 $C_2 = X_2$ (6)

FACTOR MARKETS

Demand

$$k_1 = \left(\frac{w}{3r} \right)^{\frac{3}{4}} \tag{7}$$

$$K_1 = k_1 X_1 \tag{8}$$

$$k_2 = \left(\frac{w}{r} \right)^{\frac{1}{2}} \tag{9}$$

$$K_2 = k_2 X_2 \tag{10}$$

$$l_1 = \left(\frac{3r}{w} \right)^{\frac{1}{4}} \tag{11}$$

$$L_1 = l_1 X_1 \tag{12}$$

$$l_2 = \left(\frac{r}{w} \right)^{\frac{1}{2}} \tag{13}$$

$$L_2 = l_2 X_2 \tag{14}$$

Market clearing $K_1 + K_2 = K^\star$ (15)
                 $L_1 + L_2 = L^\star$ (16)

CONSUMER'S INCOME

$$Y = r(K_1 + K_2) + w(L_1 + L_2) \tag{17}$$

The 17 endogenous variables are $C_1\ C_2\ X_1\ X_2\ K_1\ K_2\ L_1\ L_2$
                                     $k_1\ k_2\ l_1\ l_2\ P_1\ P_2\ w\ r\ Y$
The variables $K^\star$ and $L^\star$ are exogenous.

---

somewhat different structure for the computer program required to solve the general equilibrium system.

As explained in Chapter 2, any one of the four prices can be normalised at unity; in this model it is convenient to use one of the factor prices, so in the program we set $W = 1$. This means that the relative prices emerging in the general equilibrium solution are measured in terms of labour units; the price of commodity 1, for example, shows how many units of labour would exchange for one unit of good 1. In the computer programs written to solve the model of Chapter 2 one price was normalised at unity and the three remaining prices were INPUT to start the iteration procedure; when writing the computer program to solve for the equilibrium values of the model in Table 4.1, only one price need be INPUT after the initial normalisation. If we normalise by setting $W = 1$, and then INPUT a value for R, the per unit factor demands are determined, and hence the commodity prices are determined from the unit price equations.

In the computer program presented as Table 4.2 the per unit factor demand functions (equations 7, 9, 11 and 13 from Table 4.1) are represented by the variable names UK1, UK2, UL1 and UL2. A programming problem arises because the total demands for the factors K1, K2, L1, and L2 are functions of the levels of output X1 and X2. In the program of Table 2.1, written to solve the model with decreasing returns to scale, the values of X1 and X2 were determined from the firms' supply functions, but given the absence

Table 4.2 Computer Program for the Constant Returns to Scale Model

```
 10 REM GENERAL EQUILIBRIUM TWO-GOOD MODEL WITH CONSTANT
    RETURNS TO SCALE
 20 REM SUGGESTED INPUT VALUES: R=1.55, X1=0.85
 30 LET K = 0.8
 40 LET L = 2.0
 50 LET W = 1
 60 INPUT "INITIAL VALUE FOR R?  " R
 70 INPUT "INITIAL VALUE FOR X1? " X1
 80 LET UK1 = (W/(3*R))^0.75
 90 LET UK2 = (W/R)^0.5
100 LET UL1 = ((3*R)/W)^0.25
110 LET UL2 = (R/W)^0.5
120 LET P1 = R*UK1+W*UL1
130 LET P2 = R*UK2+W*UL2
```

```
140 LET L1 = X1*UL1
150 LET L2 = L-L1
160 LET X2 = L2/UL2
170 LET K1 = X1*UK1
180 LET K2 = X2*UK2
190 LET Y = R*(K1+K2)+W*(L1+L2)
200 LET C1 = Y/(2*P1)
210 LET C2 = Y/(2*P2)
220 LET X1 = C1
230 IF  ABS(K-K1-K2)<0.01 THEN GOTO 310
240 IF (K1+K2)>K THEN PRINT "EXCESS DEMAND FOR CAPITAL"
250 IF (K1+K2)>K THEN LET R = R+.001
260 IF (K1+K2)<K THEN PRINT "EXCESS SUPPLY OF CAPITAL"
270 IF (K1+K2)<K THEN LET R = R-.001
280 PRINT "R = "R
290 PRINT
300 GOTO 80
310 PRINT "EQUILIBRIUM PRICES"
320 PRINT "P1 = "P1
330 PRINT "P2 = "P2
340 PRINT "R = "R
350 PRINT "W = "W
360 PRINT
370 PRINT "EQUILIBRIUM OUTPUT AND EMPLOYMENT"
380 PRINT "X1 = "X1
390 PRINT "X2 = "X2
400 PRINT "K1 = "K1
410 PRINT "K2 = "K2
420 PRINT "L1 = "L1
430 PRINT "L2 = "L2
440 PRINT
450 PRINT "CHECK WALRAS' LAW"
460 PRINT "C2 = "C2, "X2 = "X2
```

of supply functions in the constant returns to scale model, the levels of output cannot be derived simply from knowing the relative prices in the system. This problem is dealt with in the following way: an initial value for the output of firm 1, X1, is INPUT, and used as the basis for calculating the factor demand L1 (line 140); line 150 of the program then uses the labour market clearing equation (equation 16) to determine how much labour is left for use by firm 2. The model equation (14) which gives the relation between the amount of labour demanded by firm 2 and the level of output of firm 2 can be solved for X2 and used to provide line 160 of the program. The demands for the factor capital can then be derived, using these provisional levels of output; and the consumer's income and demand for the two commodities can be calculated. The iteration procedure for this model consists of an adjustment in the capital market with R increasing or decreasing in response to the excess demand or supply of capital. Market clearing for good 1 is imposed by the line 220

220 LET X1 = C1

which provides a new value for X1 in the next round of the iteration. The market clearing equation for good 2 is not used but is satisfied by Walras' Law. As before, we include a PRINT statement for the omitted market in order to check that the program has run correctly.

When this program is RUN the equilibrium values are seen to be

P1 = 1.95	X1 = 0.82	K1 = 0.26	L1 = 1.20
P2 = 2.46	X2 = 0.65	K2 = 0.53	L2 = 0.80
R = 1.52			
W = 1			

4.3 An Input–Output Model

It was shown in the preceeding chapter that inter-industry flows can be incorporated in a two-sector model by assuming a Leontief system with fixed input-output coefficients. The general equilibrium model has to be adapted by including the inter-industry flows in the commodity balance equations, and by including the cost of intermediate inputs in the unit price equations; the relevant equations are those numbered (3.27), (3.28), (3.35) and (3.36) in the previous chapter. In this section we set out the equations for a general equilibrium model in which we assume that the value added component of the firms' production functions can be described by the same Cobb-Douglas functions as those used for the firms' production functions in the model of the previous section. This means that the conditional factor demands are the same as in that model — only equations (3), (4), (5) and (6) differ between the models of Table 4.1 and Table 4.3. In Table 4.3, a_{ij} represents the (constant) proportion of the output of industry j contributed by industry i.

Adapting the two-sector model to include inter-industry flows

Table 4.3 An Input-Output Model

COMMODITY MARKETS

Demand
$$C_1 = \frac{Y}{2P_1} \tag{1}$$

$$C_2 = \frac{Y}{2P_2} \tag{2}$$

Unit price
equations
$$P_1 = a_{11}P_1 + a_{21}P_2 + rk_1 + wl_1 \tag{3}$$
$$P_2 = a_{12}P_1 + a_{22}P_2 + rk_2 + wl_2 \tag{4}$$

Commodity
balance
$$X_1 = a_{11}X_1 + a_{12}X_2 + C_1 \tag{5}$$
$$X_2 = a_{21}X_1 + a_{22}X_2 + C_2 \tag{6}$$

FACTOR MARKETS

Demand
$$k_1 = \left(\frac{w}{3r}\right)^{\frac{3}{4}} \tag{7}$$

$$K_1 = k_1 X_1 \tag{8}$$

$$k_2 = \left(\frac{w}{r}\right)^{\frac{1}{2}} \tag{9}$$

$$K_2 = k_2 X_2 \tag{10}$$

$$l_1 = \left(\frac{3r}{w}\right)^{\frac{1}{4}} \tag{11}$$

$$L_1 = l_1 X_1 \tag{12}$$

$$l_2 = \left(\frac{r}{w}\right)^{\frac{1}{2}} \tag{13}$$

$$L_2 = l_2 X_2 \tag{14}$$

Market clearing
$$K_1 + K_2 = K^\star \tag{15}$$
$$L_1 + L_2 = L^\star \tag{16}$$

CONSUMER'S INCOME

$$Y = r(K_1 + K_2) + w(L_1 + L_2) \tag{17}$$

The 17 endogenous variables are C_1 C_2 X_1 X_2 K_1 K_2 L_1 L_2
k_1 k_2 l_1 l_2 P_1 P_2 w r Y

The variables a_{11}, a_{12}, a_{21}, a_{22}, $K^\star$ and $L^\star$ are exogenous.

---

along the lines described in Chapter 3 does not present any serious difficulty. The changed structure of the model does, however, complicate the writing of the computer program to solve the system. The reason why this model is harder to program for a solution can be understood by examining equations (3), (4), (5) and (6) in Table 4.3. It will be seen that the equation defining P_1 includes P_2 as an explanatory variable; similarly the equation defining P_2 includes P_1. There is therefore a problem of simultaneity in determining the value of the price variables, and the same problem arises with the output variables X_1 and X_2 which both appear in equations (5) and (6).

The computer program for the previous constant returns to scale model began by normalising W at unity; a value for the rental on capital R was then INPUT, and the unit price equations (equations 3 and 4 in Table 4.1) were used to find the values of P1 and P2. We cannot proceed so directly in the present model because P_1 and P_2 appear in both the unit price equations. Before the computer program for Table 4.3 can be written, the two pairs of simultaneous equations in P_1 and P_2, X_1 and X_2 have to be solved, to find the price variables in terms of r and w and the (exogenous) input coefficients, and to find the output variables in terms of the final demands, C_1 and C_2, and the input coefficients. Re-writing equations (3) and (4) of Table 5.2 with the product price terms on the left gives

$$(1-a_{11})P_1 - a_{21}P_2 = rK_1 + wl_1$$
$$-a_{12}P_1 + (1-a_{22})P_2 = rk_2 + wl_2$$

and solving these two simultaneous equations for P_1 and P_2:

$$P_1 = [(1-a_{22})\,(rk_1+wl_1) + a_{21}(rk_2+wl_2)] / A \qquad (4.17)$$
$$P_2 = [(1-a_{11})\,(rk_2+wl_2) + a_{12}(rk_1+wl_1)] / A \qquad (4.18)$$

where

$$A = (1-a_{11})\,(1-a_{22})-a_{12}a_{21}$$

In the same way re-writing equations (5) and (6) as

$$(1-a_{11})X_1 - a_{12}X_2 = C_1$$
$$-a_{21}X_1 + (1-a_{22})X_2 = C_2$$

and solving for X_1 and X_2 gives

$$X_1 = [(1-a_{22})C_1 + a_{12}C_2] / A \qquad (4.19)$$
$$X_2 = [(1-a_{11})C_2 + a_{21}C_1] / A \qquad (4.20)$$

where A is defined as above. The reader will see that equations

(4.19) and (4.20) represent the specific equations corresponding to the general solution of the Leontief input-output model (equation (3.30) in the previous chapter).

$$X = (I - A)^{-1}C$$

The rather cumbersome expressions (4.17) – (4.20) have to be used in writing the computer program to solve the model of Table 4.3. Before writing the program, values have to be assigned to the (exogenously determined) inter-industry input coefficients: we assume $a_{11} = 0.05$, $a_{12} = 0.20$, $a_{21} = 0.15$, $a_{22} = 0.10$, and use the names A11, A12, A21, and A22 for these variables in the program. The structure of the program is similar to that of Table 4.2; having normalised by setting $W = 1$, initial values are supplied for X1 and R, and the iteration procedure consists of searching for the market-clearing price in the capital market. The only difference between the program of Table 4.2 and the program in Table 4.4 comes from using equations (4.17) and (4.18) to define P1 and P2, and using equations (4.19) and (4.20) to define X1 and X2. It will be noted that when checking Walras' Law in the omitted market for good 2, the market clearing equation no longer requires X2 to be equal to C2, but rather to the right-hand side of equation (4.20), defined in line 520 of the program as D2.

Table 4.4 Computer Program for the Input-Output Model

```
10 REM GENERAL EQUILIBRIUM TWO-GOOD MODEL WITH
   CONSTANT RETURNS TO SCALE AND INTER-INDUSTRY FLOWS.
20 REM SUGGESTED INPUT VALUES: R=1.5, X1=0.8
30 LET K = 0.8
40 LET L = 2.0
50 LET A11 = 0.05
60 LET A12 = 0.20
70 LET A21 = 0.15
80 LET A22 = 0.10
90 LET A = (1-A11)*(1-A22)-A12*A21
100 LET W = 1
110 INPUT "INITIAL VALUE FOR R?  " R
120 INPUT "INITIAL VALUE FOR X1? " X1
130 LET UK1 = (W/(3*R))^0.75
140 LET UK2 = (W/R)^0.5
150 LET UL1 = ((3*R)/W)^0.25
160 LET UL2 = (R/W)^0.5
```

```
170 LET P1 = ((1-A22)*(R*UK1+W*UL1) +
    A21*(R*UK2+W*UL2)) / A
180 LET P2 = ((1-A11)*(R*UK2+W*UL2) +
    A12*(R*UK1+W*UL1)) / A
190 LET L1 = X1*UL1
200 LET L2 = L-L1
210 LET X2 = L2/UL2
220 LET K1 = X1*UK1
230 LET K2 = X2*UK2
240 LET Y = R*(K1+K2)+W*(L1+L2)
250 LET C1 = Y/(2*P1)
260 LET C2 = Y/(2*P2)
270 LET X1 = ((1-A22)*C1+A12*C2)/A
280 IF ABS(K-K1-K2)<0.001 THEN GOTO 360
290 IF (K1+K2)>K THEN PRINT "EXCESS DEMAND FOR CAPITAL"
300 IF (K1+K2)>K THEN LET R = R+.001
310 IF (K1+K2)<K THEN PRINT "EXCESS SUPPLY OF CAPITAL"
320 IF (K1+K2)<K THEN LET R = R-.001
330 PRINT "R = "R
340 PRINT
350 GOTO 130
360 PRINT
370 PRINT "EQUILIBRIUM PRICES"
380 PRINT "P1 = "P1
390 PRINT "P2 = "P2
400 PRINT "R = "R
410 PRINT "W = "W
420 PRINT
430 PRINT "EQUILIBRIUM OUTPUT AND EMPLOYMENT"
440 PRINT "X1 = "X1
450 PRINT "X2 = "X2
460 PRINT "K1 = "K1
470 PRINT "K2 = "K2
480 PRINT "L1 = "L1
490 PRINT "L2 = "L2
500 PRINT
510 PRINT "CHECK WALRAS' LAW"
520 LET D2 = ((1-A11)*C2+A21*C1)/A
530 PRINT "D2 = "D2, "X2 = "X2
```

Table 4.4 shows the computer program for the input-output model.
When this program is RUN the equilibrium values are seen to be

P1 = 2.58	X1 = 0.80	K1 = 0.26	L1 = 1.17
P2 = 3.32	X2 = 0.67	K2 = 0.54	L2 = 0.83
R = 1.52	C1 = 0.63		
W = 1	C2 = 0.49		

5

THE OPEN ECONOMY

5.1 Introduction to the Open Economy Model

The general equilibrium models presented in the text so far have been very simple models of a closed economy. In this chapter and the next we retain the basic framework of the model with its one consumer, two goods and two factors, and show how the model can be extended to include foreign trade and government intervention in the economy. The open economy model of this chapter is related to the elementary theory of international trade. After a brief introductory discussion about the consequences of introducing trade into a previously closed economy, a formal general model including imports and exports is constructed in Section 5.2, with a specific numerical example in Section 5.3. The last two sections of the chapter use the numerical example as a basis for considering the role played by relative world prices and relative factor endowments in establishing patterns of production and trade in the open economy. The Rybczynski theorem and the Heckscher-Ohlin theorem are illustrated using specific models solved by computer programs. Further examples illustrating trade theory will be found in Chapter 7, after the introduction of the public sector in Chapter 6.

Once foreign trade is included in the model the 'closed' economy becomes an 'open' economy, and the circular flow diagram takes the form shown in Figure 5.1.

With the addition of exports and imports there is a new dimension of choice for consumers and producers: imports provide an alternative source of supply for the consumer, and exports constitute an additional source of demand for the firms' products. In the case of the two-sector model, the consequences for the commodity markets of opening up the economy to trade can be represented diagrammatically (Figures 5.2 and 5.3).

In Figure 5.2, *AB* is the transformation curve which shows the domestic rate of transformation between good 1 and good 2 as more of one, and less of the other, is produced. If the two

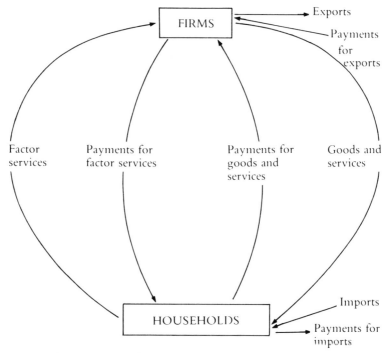

Figure 5.1 Circular Flow Diagram for the Open Economy

production functions have different factor intensities, the trans-formation curve will be concave to the origin even if there are constant returns to scale. In the absence of trade, the transformation curve shows the maximum combinations of the two goods available for consumption. Maximisation of the consumer's utility, represented by the indifference curves U_i, leads to production and consumption of the two commodities at the point Q. The tangent of the line at the point Q, which measures the marginal rate of transformation of the two goods at the optimum point, will reflect the ratio of the relative prices P_1/P_2. With the opening up of the economy to trade with the rest of the world, the country has the option of buying goods abroad at their world price, or of exporting part of the economy's output at the world price. If the ratio of the world prices, which we shall denote by P_{W1} and $P_{W2}2$, differs from the pre-trade domestic price ratio, the consumer will be able to exploit the potential gains from trade. The new situation is illustrated in Figure 5.3.

With trade the consumer is able to move to point T on a higher indifference curve U_2 where the quantities C_1 and C_2 can be consumed. Domestic production is now at point R and the gaps between production and consumption of the two goods represent the quantities either imported or exported. Which good is imported and which exported will depend upon the relative world prices P_{W1}/P_{W2}, represented in Figure 5.3 by the slope of the line SS. In this diagram good 1 is exported and good 2 is imported. Using E to denote exports and M to denote imports:

$$E = X_1 - C_1 \tag{5.1}$$
$$M = C_2 - X_2 \tag{5.2}$$

Some of the consequences of the move from self-sufficiency to trade are illustrated: the level of consumption is no longer constrained to be the same as the level of production, and the

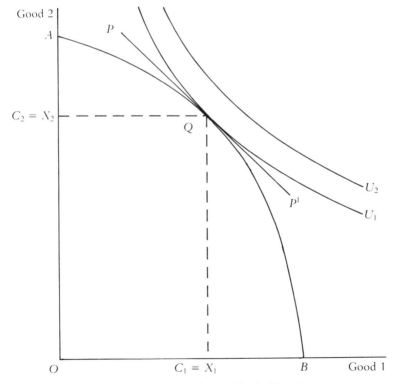

Figure 5.2 The Pre-Trade Situation

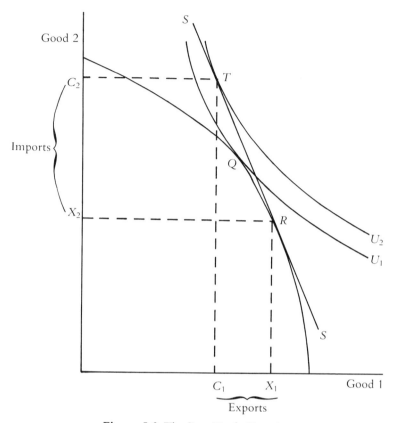

Figure 5.3 The Post-Trade Situation

consumer is able to move to a preferred position on a higher indifference curve. The marginal rate of transformation between the two goods, which previously reflected the pre-trade domestic price ratio, now reflects the world price ratio adopted by the domestic economy as a result of free trade.

The choice of new levels of domestic production X_1 and X_2 has, however, further consequences. If the factor proportions used in industry 1 and industry 2 vary, the movement of resources from one industry to another will mean that there are shifts in the demand for the two factors of production, and the returns to each factor will be affected by the introduction of trade into the two-good economy. Separate diagrams can be drawn to illustrate the consequences of trade on the factor markets, but these diagrams require implicit assumptions about the firms' production functions which are not evident from Figures 5.2 and 5.3. An advantage of the approach used in this book is that by formulating the complete general equilibrium model, the interconnections between the product and factor markets are clearly laid out. A further advantage is that relations between foreign and domestic prices, and the significance of the balance of payments constraint are made evident. We therefore proceed to formulate a full general equilibrium model for the open economy and then to construct a specific numerical example of the general model. This example is used in the following sections to illustrate some general propositions from trade theory; but it should be borne in mind that one of the principal uses of a numerical example is that it can readily be changed. Some of the results inherent in the general equilibrium solution to the model provided by the computer program are sensitive to the choice of parameters used; others are not. The discussion in Section 5.4 examines some of these questions, and a number of exercises are suggested which throw further light upon the assumptions commonly made in the orthodox presentation of international trade theory.

5.2   The Open Economy Model

We speak in this section of 'the' open economy model. There are, of course, many ways in which the open economy can be modelled. In formulating the equations of the model of this section we shall make and discuss a number of assumptions about the nature of the open economy model presented.

   The first assumption we make in the model of this section is that the economy engaging in world trade is presented with a given set of world prices which will not be affected by the country's level of exports and imports. This is the assumption known in the language of trade theory as the 'small country' assumption, and contrasts with the 'large country' assumption which states that world prices will be affected by the country's trading activities. (We consider a way of modelling the 'large country' assumption in Chapter 7.) It will be noted that although the model we present in this section is a general equilibrium model for the economy concerned, it is only a partial equilibrium model from the point of view of the world as a whole. A global model would show how international prices are determined, and a development of the analysis of this section will be found in Section 5.5 which introduces a second country and demonstrates the implications for the determination of world prices.

The open economy model includes two sets of prices, world prices and domestic prices, and a new variable, the exchange rate, has to be introduced to provide a link between the two. In the free trade economy, with no taxes or other restrictions on trade, the relation between the two sets of prices is straightforward: world prices must be multiplied by the exchange rate to convert them into domestic prices. Using F to represent the exchange rate, we have the following two equations:

$$P_1 = FP_{W1} \tag{5.3}$$
$$P_2 = FP_{W2} \tag{5.4}$$

As noted above, P_{W1} and P_{W2} are treated as exogenous variables in a 'small' open economy, but F is an endogenous variable, and must be added to the list of relative prices in the general equilibrium system. We have emphasised that all prices in a general equilibrium system have to be interpreted in terms of a numeraire. F represents the price of one unit of foreign purchasing power, and can be determined using either of the goods or either of the factors as numeraire. Alternatively, F can be normalised at 1, and the domestic prices are then calculated relative to the value of traded goods.

In order to convert the closed economy model of the earlier chapters into an open economy model, the equations (5.1) – (5.4) must be incorporated in the system. One further equation is required; imports and exports, M and E, have been introduced into the commodity balance equations (5.1) and (5.2); but the relation between these two variables has not been defined. For general equilibrium, if capital flows are excluded from the model, total expenditure on imports must equal total earnings from exports:

$$P_{W1}M - P_{W2}E = 0 \tag{5.5}$$

This equation may be described as the balance of payments equation or the foreign exchange constraint for the economy.

We are now able to present the full general equilibrium open economy model. Either the decreasing returns to scale model of Chapter 1 or the constant returns to scale models of Chapter 3 can be adapted by replacing the commodity market clearing equations by (5.1) and (5.2), and by adding the three equations (5.3) – (5.5) to the system. It will be noted that there are three new equations, and three new variables in the open economy version of the general equilibrium model: M, E and F. As the usual 2×2 international trade model assumes constant returns to scale we base our open economy model, presented as Table 5.1, on the closed economy model given in Table 3.1.

Table 5.1 Open Economy Model with Constant Returns to Scale

COMMODITY MARKETS

Demand	$C_1 = C_1(P_1, P_2, Y)$	(1)
	$C_2 = C_2(P_1, P_2, Y)$	(2)
Unit price equations	$P_1 = rk_1 + wl_1$	(3)
	$P_2 = rk_2 + wl_2$	(4)
Market clearing	$C_1 = X_1 - E$	(5)
	$C_2 = X_2 + M$	(6)

FACTOR MARKETS

Demand	$k_1 = k_1(r,w)$	(7)
	$K_1 = k_1 X_1$	(8)
	$k_2 = k_2(r,w)$	(9)
	$K_2 = k_2 X_2$	(10)
	$l_1 = l_1(r,w)$	(11)
	$L_1 = l_1 X_1$	(12)
	$l_2 = k_2(r,w)$	(13)
	$L_2 = l_2 X_2$	(14)
Market clearing	$K_1 + K_2 = K^\star$	(15)
	$L_1 + L_2 = L^\star$	(16)

CONSUMER'S INCOME

$$Y = r(K_1+K_2) + w(L_1+L_2) \qquad (17)$$

FOREIGN SECTOR

Price equations	$P_1 = FP_{W1}$	(18)
	$P_1 = FP_{W2}$	(19)
Balance of payments constraint	$P_{W1}E - P_{W2}M = 0$	(20)

The 20 endogenous variables are C_1 C_2 X_1 X_2 K_1 K_2 L_1 L_2 k_1 k_2 l_1 l_2 P_1 P_2 w r Y E M F
The variables $K^\star$ $L^\star$ P_{W1} P_{W2} are exogenous.

The model of Table 5.1 has a characteristic which distinguishes it from the models encountered earlier in the book. It is a fixed-price, not a flexible-price model. This feature of the model is the consequence of combining the assumption of fixed world prices with the assumption of constant returns to scale in production. If we consider the equations of the above model with the normalisation $F = 1$, it is obvious from equations (18) and (19) that the exogenously determined world prices P_{W1} and P_{W2} will fix the domestic prices P_1 and P_2. Examination of the unit price equations (3) and (4) will show that once P_1 and P_2 have been determined, the factor prices are also fixed. P_1 and P_2 are both functions of r and w; when P_1 and P_2 are set at their internationally determined levels, the unit price equations can be seen to be a pair of simultaneous equations in the variables r and w. Solving these equations for r and w provides the (unique) values for the price of capital and the price of labour in the model.

With fixed prices the market clearing assumptions of the previous models no longer hold. With flexible prices we have been able to make the assumption (which has been incorporated in the numerical examples) that excess demand will lead to rising prices, and excess supply will lead to falling prices. In the fixed price model market clearing can only be brought about by quantity adjustments; this will be demonstrated in the numerical example of the next section. A fixed price model presents different problems from one with freely adjusting market prices and we shall discuss this issue with the aid of the numerical example in Section 5.4. Further considerations about fixed and flexible price models will be found in Chapter 8, Section 8.2.

5.3   The Open Economy: A Numerical Example

The numerical example of this section is based on the constant returns to scale model of Chapter 4 with the addition of the three variables and three equations needed to convert the closed economy to an open economy. Table 5.2 is therefore a specific example of the model in Table 5.1 which uses the demand and supply functions derived in the earlier chapters.

As noted at the end of the previous section the two-good, two-factor open economy model of a 'small' country, with constant returns to scale is characterised by fixed prices. Once any one of the five prices in the model, P_1, P_2, r, w, or F, has been normalised at

Table 5.2 A Numerical Example of the Open Economy Model

COMMODITY MARKETS

Demand $C_1 = \dfrac{Y}{2P_1}$ (1)

                                    $C_2 = \dfrac{Y}{2P_2}$ (2)

Unit price equations $P_1 = rk_1 + wl_1$ (3)
                                    $P_2 = rk_2 + wl_2$ (4)

Market clearing $C_1 = X_1 - E$ (5)
                                    $C_2 = X_2 + M$ (6)

FACTOR MARKETS

Demand

$$k_1 = \left(\frac{w}{3r}\right)^{\frac{3}{4}}$$ (7)

$$K_1 = k_1 X_1$$ (8)

$$k_2 = \left(\frac{w}{r}\right)^{\frac{1}{2}}$$ (9)

$$K_2 = k_2 X_2$$ (10)

$$l_1 = \left(\frac{3r}{w}\right)^{\frac{1}{4}}$$ (11)

$$L_1 = l_1 X_1$$ (12)

$$l_2 = \left(\frac{r}{w}\right)^{\frac{1}{2}}$$ (13)

$$L_2 = l_2 X_2$$ (14)

Market clearing $K_1 + K_2 = K^\star$ (15)
                                    $L_1 + L_2 = L^\star$ (16)

CONSUMER'S INCOME

                          $Y = r(K_1 + K_2) + w(L_1 + L_2)$ (17)

FOREIGN SECTOR

Price equations $P_1 = FP_{W1}$ (18)
                                    $P_1 = FP_{W2}$ (19)

Balance of payments $P_{W1}E - P_{W2}M = 0$ (20)
constraint

The 20 endogenous variables are C_1 C_2 X_1 X_2 K_1 K_2 L_1 L_2
k_1 k_2 l_1 l_2 P_1 P_2 w r Y E M F

The variables $K^\star$ $L^\star$ P_{W1} P_{W2} are exogenous.

---

unity, the four remaining prices are determined by equations (3), (4), (18), and (19). This means that the market price iteration procedure used to solve all the computer programs discussed so far cannot be used for this model. Finding a solution that ensures all markets clear involves the use of the factor market clearing equations and the factor demand equations to establish the necessary conditions for full employment in the factor markets. Fulfilment of these necessary conditions will determine a given level of output of X_1 and X_2. General equilibrium will prevail when these full-employment levels of output are equal to the total demand for the two commodities, including both domestic and foreign demand.

For the factor markets to clear, the demand for capital and labour by the two firms must just equal the supply of the factors. The factor demand functions (equations 8, 10, 12 and 14 in Table 5.2) are determined by the level of output of the firm and the per unit factor requirements k_1 and l_1, which are, in their turn, functions of r and w. By substituting the factor demand functions into the factor market clearing equations (15) and (16), we have a pair of equations from which we can solve for the levels of output, X_1 and X_2, that generate full employment.

$$l_1X_1 + l_2X_2 = L^\star \tag{5.6}$$
$$k_1X_1 + k_2X_2 = K^\star \tag{5.7}$$

The solutions to (5.6) and (5.7) are given by

$$X_1 = (k_2L^\star - l_2K^\star) / A \tag{5.8}$$
$$X_2 = (l_1K^\star - k_1L^\star) / A \tag{5.9}$$

where $A = l_1k_2 - k_1l_2$. Equations (5.8) and (5.9) provide the values for X_1 and X_2 which jointly ensure full employment in the factor markets. Each output variable is expressed in terms of the initial factor endowments $K^\star$ and $L^\star$, and the per unit factor demands which are in turn functions of the factor prices r and w; the next problem, therefore, is to determine the values of r and w in this open economy model. We noted earlier that when P_1 and P_2 are known, the unit price equations (equations (3) and (4) in Table 5.2) can be solved for r and w. By substituting for the per unit factor requirements in these equations

$$P_1 = r\left(\frac{w}{3r}\right)^{\frac{3}{4}} + w\left(\frac{3r}{w}\right)^{\frac{1}{4}}$$

$$P_2 = r\left(\frac{w}{r}\right)^{\frac{1}{2}} + w\left(\frac{r}{w}\right)^{\frac{1}{2}}$$

The pair of equations can be solved for r and w in terms of P_1 and P_2. The algebra involved is tedious but straightforward, and the reader can check that by solving each of the two equations for one of the factor prices and equating the resulting expressions, a value for the other factor price can be established in terms of P_1 and P_2. Solving in this way for each of the factor prices we have:

$$r = \frac{P_2^3\left[\left(\frac{1}{3}\right)^{\frac{3}{4}} + 3^{\frac{1}{4}}\right]^2}{8P_1^2} \tag{5.10}$$

$$w = \frac{2P_1^2}{P_2\left[\left(\frac{1}{3}\right)^{\frac{3}{4}} + 3^{\frac{1}{4}}\right]^2} \tag{5.11}$$

It is now possible, after these algebraic preliminaries, to write a computer program to solve the equilibrium system defined by the equations of Table 5.2. As usual, any one of the five prices can be normalised at unity. In this program we follow a common convention in open economy models and set the exchange rate $F = 1$. The world prices are exogenous variables in the 'small' country model and we choose the arbitrary values $P_{W1} = 1.4$, $P_{w2} = 1.6$.[1]

The structure of the program in Table 5.3 is as follows. First, the exogenous variables are defined; then the normalisation sets $F = 1$,

---

1. In open economy general equilibrium models it is common to define units of the traded goods in such a way that all foreign prices can be set equal to unity. We do not use this convention for pedagogic reasons, as it is important to distinguish between the normalisation by which one of the relative prices in the general equilibrium system is set equal to unity, and the arbitrary values assigned to the exogenously determined world prices.

enabling all the other prices to be defined using the equations (18) and (19) from Table 5.2 for P1 and P2, and the equations (5.10) and (5.11) for R and W; the per unit factor requirements are then defined in terms of R and W, and the full employment levels of X1 and X2 calculated using equations (5.7) and (5.8); factor demands, consumer income and commodity demand functions are as in previous models, and the open economy market clearing equations (equations (5) and (6) in Table 5.2) are used to determine values for exports E and imports M. Equation (20) of the model in Table 5.2, which defines the balance of payments constraint, is not used in the program, but is satisfied by Walras' Law. If the program runs correctly, it will be seen that the value of the balance of payments (defined as the variable BP in line 270 of the program) is equal to zero.

Table 5.3 Computer Program to Solve Open Economy Model

```
 10 REM OPEN ECONOMY MODEL WITH CONSTANT RETURNS
 20 LET K = 0.8
 30 LET L = 2.0
 40 LET PW1 = 1.4
 50 LET PW2 = 1.6
 60 LET F = 1
 70 LET P1 = F*PW1
 80 LET P2 = F*PW2
 90 LET R = (P2^3*((1/3)^0.75+3^0.25)^2)/(8*P1^2)
100 LET W = (2*P1^2)/(P2*((1/3)^0.75+3^0.25)^2)
110 LET UK1 = (W/(3*R))^0.75
120 LET UK2 = (W/R)^0.5
130 LET UL1 = ((3*R)/W)^0.25
140 LET UL2 = (R/W)^0.5
150 LET A = UL1*UK2-UL2*UK1
160 LET X1 = (L*UK2-K*UL2)/A
170 LET X2 = (K*UL1-L*UK1)/A
180 LET K1 = UK1*X1
190 LET K2 = UK2*X2
200 LET L1 = UL1*X1
210 LET L2 = UL2*X2
220 LET Y = R*(K1+K2)+W*(L1+L2)
230 LET C1 = Y/(2*P1)
240 LET C2 = Y/(2*P2)
250 LET M = C2-X2
260 LET E = X1-C1
270 LET BP = (PW1*E-PW2*M)
```

```
280 PRINT
290 PRINT "EQUILIBRIUM PRICES"
300 PRINT "P1 = "P1
310 PRINT "P2 = "P2
320 PRINT "R = "R
330 PRINT "W = "W
340 PRINT "F = "F
350 PRINT
360 PRINT "EQUILIBRIUM OUTPUT AND EMPLOYMENT"
370 PRINT "X1 = "X1
380 PRINT "X2 = "X2
390 PRINT "K1 = "K1
400 PRINT "K2 = "K2
410 PRINT "L1 = "L1
420 PRINT "L2 = "L2
430 PRINT
440 PRINT "FOREIGN SECTOR"
450 PRINT "E = "E
460 PRINT "M = "M
470 PRINT "BP = "BP
```

It will be noted that the program in Table 5.3 has no iteration procedure. As all domestic prices are determined by the (exogenous) values of world prices in the constant returns to scale model there is no mechanism for adjusting prices in response to excess supply or excess demand. The full employment solution is imposed on the model by incorporating both factor market and both commodity market clearing equations in the structure of the program. The equilibrium values that result when this program is run are as follows:

$P1 = 1.4$	$X1 = 1.35$	$X2 = 0.21$	$E = 0.56$
$P2 = 1.6$	$K1 = 0.59$	$K2 = 0.21$	$M = 0.49$
$R = 0.80$	$L1 = 1.79$	$L2 = 0.21$	
$W = 0.80$			
$F = 1$			

We comment on some features of this solution in the next section.

5.4 Factor Endowments, World Prices, Production and Trade

The solution to the model of the previous section showed that in the open economy version of the constant returns to scale model, both goods were produced domestically and both entered world trade — good 1 as an export and good 2 as an import. This result would not necessarily follow for a two-sector economy opened up to world trade. We have emphasised that with constant returns to scale and the 'small' country assumption all prices are fixed in the model. With the particular parameters chosen, the commodity prices and the factor prices were such that both industries remained profitable in the post-trade situation even though part of the requirement of good 2 is now met from abroad. The choice of other values for the exogenous variables, the initial factor endowments and the world prices, could lead to a different outcome.

We consider first the consequences of different factor endowments at the given set of world prices. In the model of Table 5.2 industry 1 is relatively labour-intensive, industry 2 is relatively capital-intensive. This can be seen by calculating the capital-labour ratios for each firm: in the solution to the general equilibrium system described by the above model, $K_1 = 0.59$, $L_1 = 1.79$; $K_2 = 0.21$, $L_2 = 0.21$ (to 2 decimal places); the capital-labour ratios calculated to 2 decimal places are $K_1/L_1 = 0.33$; $K_2/L_2 = 0.99$. In the solution to the model the labour-intensive good is exported and the capital-intensive good is imported. What would be the consequence of altering the assumptions made about the initial factor endowments? The answer to this question is familiar to international trade theorists, and can be very clearly illustrated by using the computer program of Table 5.3, and running the program using different values for the values of K and L at lines 20 and 30. The results of three such computer 'experiments' are presented in Table 5.4. The first column gives the values of production and trade for the original 'base' program of Table 5.3; the second column shows the consequences of assuming an increase in the supply of capital; and the third column shows the consequences of increasing the initial endowment of labour.

Table 5.4 shows that an increase in the supply of capital leads to an increase in the domestic production of the production of the capital-intensive good, good 2, and a drop in the production of the labour-intensive good, good 1. Fewer imports of good 2 are now required, and the level of trade drops. With an increase in the supply of labour, however, these consequences are reversed: the production of the labour-intensive good 1 is increased and the production of good 2 drops; with the fall in the production of good 2, imports rise and are paid for by a higher level of exports of good 1. These numbers illustrate the Rybczynski theorem which states:

Table 5.4 Consequences of Changing Initial Factor Endowments

K = 0.8, L = 2.0	K = 1.0, L = 2.0	K = 0.8, L = 2.2
X1 = 1.35	X1 = 1.12	X1 = 1.58
K1 = 0.59	K1 = 0.49	K1 = 0.69
L1 = 1.79	L1 = 1.48	L1 = 2.08
X2 = 0.21	X2 = 0.51	X2 = 0.11
K2 = 0.21	K2 = 0.51	K2 = 0.11
L2 = 0.21	L2 = 0.51	L2 = 0.11
E = 0.56	E = 0.26	E = 0.72
M = 0.49	M = 0.24	M = 0.64

If one of the factors of production increases, the other one being held constant, the output of the good using the accumulating factor intensively will increase and the output of the other will decrease in absolute amount, provided that commodity prices and factor prices are held constant. (Sodersten, 1980)

In addition to illustrating the Rybczynski theorem, this numerical example provokes further questions. The third column shows that as the supply of labour increases, and production of the labour-intensive export good, good 1, increases, production of the capital-intensive good falls. Further computer 'experiments' will show that if the initial endowment of labour is increased further, industry 2 will be eliminated, and all the economy's requirements of good 2 will be met by imports. If, on the other hand, the original value for L is assumed and the supply of capital is increased, industry 1 will contract and industry 2 will expand. Computer experiments will show that with L held constant at its initial value of 2.0, and the value of K steadily increased, the values for E and M will become negative as K approaches the value of 1.2. Negative values for the trade variables indicate that good 1 has now become an import, and good 2 an export. Further increases in the value of K, holding L constant, will lead to the eventual elimination of industry 1, as the production of the capital-intensive good 2 becomes relatively more and more profitable at the prevailing world prices.

If the initial factor endowments are such that one industry is eliminated by foreign trade, the structure of the model changes. The economy now specialises in the production of only one commodity, and meets its requirements of the other good by importing. As only one firm is employing the two factors of production, factor prices are no longer fixed by the two commodity prices, but will again be determined by supply and demand in the factor markets. For the open-economy two-good model to be preserved with domestic production as well as consumption of both goods, the initial factor endowments must fall within a given range of values. This set of values is known in the international trade literature as the diversification cone, and it is often implicitly assumed in the presentation of the two-sector model that the initial factor endowments fall within the diversification cone. The computer experiments suggested in this chapter show the importance of this assumption, and also show that when initial factor endowments do not fall within the diversification cone, the consequence of world trade will be specialisation in production.

The discussion so far has concentrated on the consequences of varying factor endowments given fixed world prices for the internationally traded commodities. A similar set of questions can be asked about the effects on an economy with a given set of factor endowments when world prices alter. Changing the assumptions about the world prices for good 1 and good 2 will, with the 'small' country assumption and constant returns to scale, establish new values for the domestic prices. The relative profitability of the two industries, one labour-intensive and one capital-intensive, will be affected. The particular numerical example we are using is very sensitive to changes in the relative values of the world prices. We present, in Table 5.5, figures resulting from the computer program of Table 5.2, showing what happens when first PW1 and then PW2 is increased by 0.05, with the other price remaining at its 'base' level.

Predictably, the private sector producers in the two-good economy shift resources into the production of the good with the increased price. The reader can perform further computer experiments to show that increases in the world price of good 1 rapidly lead to the elimination of industry 2. Increases in the price of the capital intensive good 2 are for a while compatible with the continued production of the labour-intensive good 1, but a constantly rising PW2 will eventually lead the economy to specialise in the production of good 2 only.

Although the results of these numerical experiments depend upon the specific values assigned to the exogenous variables and on the particular functional forms chosen for the supply and demand

Table 5.5 Consequences of Changing World Prices

PW1 = 1.4, PW2 = 1.6	PW1 = 1.45, PW2 = 1.6	PW1 = 1.4, PW2 = 1.65
X1 = 1.35	X1 = 1.53	X1 = 1.20
K1 = 0.59	K1 = 0.74	K1 = 0.47
L1 = 1.79	L1 = 1.95	L1 = 1.63
X2 = 0.21	X2 = 0.06	X2 = 0.35
K2 = 0.21	K2 = 0.06	K2 = 0.33
L2 = 0.21	L2 = 0.05	L2 = 0.37
E = 0.56	E = 0.73	E = 0.39
M = 0.49	M = 0.66	M = 0.33

functions, the exercise contains some insights of wider interest. As in the closed economy models, the use of a general equilibrium system demonstrates the interaction between the different agents in the economy and the consequences of change for the different markets. With the introduction of world trade, the initial level of factor endowments and the level of international prices are seen to exercise an important effect on the model. Once the possibility of exporting and importing is allowed for, the two-sector model may take the form described in Table 5.1, or the economy may be led to specialise in the production of only one good, for any of the reasons discussed above.

In this section we have confined ourselves to examining the consequences of varying the values of the exogenous variables. We have not considered different ways of modelling the production functions of the two firms. It is straightforward to formulate and solve an open economy version of the decreasing returns to scale model of Chapter 1, or for the input-output model of Chapter 3, and these activities are suggested as exercises for the reader. All these models are based on the use of Cobb-Douglas production functions with differing factor intensities. With the use of Cobb-Douglas production functions, it is always the case that one industry is relatively capital-intensive and one relatively labour-intensive (unless the two production functions have identical parameters, in which case there will not be a unique solution to the model). An important extension to the analysis of this chapter, but one which lies beyond the scope of the present book, would be provided by the construction of numerical examples based on CES production functions. With CES production functions the elasticity of substitution (always equal to 1 in the case of Cobb-Douglas functions) can vary, with the consequence that changes in the relative prices of the two goods can lead to factor-intensity reversals. This means that industry 1 may be relatively capital-intensive at one set of prices, and industry 2 at another set of prices. The possibility of factor-intensity reversals should be borne in mind when considering the general implications of the particular results established in this section using models in which factor-intensity reversals cannot occur.

For our last illustration of a theorem from international trade theory using the numerical example of this chapter we return to a discussion of the importance of a country's initial factor endowments.

5.5   The Heckscher-Ohlin Theorem Illustrated

The Heckscher-Ohlin theorem, which can be found in any textbook on international trade theory, states that a country will export that commodity which uses intensively its abundant factor. The following succinct statement of the two-country, two-good model used to demonstrate the theorem and known as the Heckscher-Ohlin-Samuelson model, is taken from Bhagwati and Srinivasan, 1983, p. 50:

> PRODUCTION Two factors of production; given supplies of these primary factors; constant-returns-to-scale production functions in each of the two goods; identical technical knowhow (i.e. identical production functions) in each industry internationally, and non-reversibility of factor-intensity ranking for the two commodities [. . .]
> DEMAND Balanced trade obtains, requiring that the economy spend no more than its earned income [. . .]
> TRADE No transportation costs; two countries; two traded goods; factors immobile internationally.
> INSTITUTIONAL ASSUMPTIONS Pure competition.

It will be seen that the assumptions made for each individual country in this model correspond exactly to the assumptions made for the open economy model of this chapter. With the extension to the two-country model, however, world prices become endogenous variables, determined by the supply and demand relations in the two countries taken together. It is obvious that in a two-country model the imports of one country will be the exports of the other and vice-versa. The Heckscher-Ohlin theorem predicts that the pattern of trade between otherwise identical economies will be determined by differences in initial factor endowments, each country exporting the commodity which uses intensively its relatively more abundant factor.

The full 'world' general equilibrium system for the Heckscher-Ohlin-Samuelson model described above can readily be constructed on the basis of the model in Table 5.1. With two countries, A and B, the model will consist of a duplicate set of the Table 5.1 equations for each country; the only additional feature will be two new equations stating the conditions for balanced trade — that the imports of country A should equal the exports of country B, and the imports of country B should equal the exports of country A:

$$M_A = E_B \qquad (5.12)$$
$$M_B = E_A \qquad (5.13)$$

The full equilibrium system will then consist of 42 equations in 42 variables. These will be the 20 endogenous variables of Table 5.1, duplicated for each country, and the two world prices P_{W1} and P_{W2} which will be determined by the equilibrium conditions imposed by (5.12) and (5.13) above.

For a numerical example, we can use the specific relations of Table 5.2, again duplicated for each country, Country A and Country B, and including (5.12) and (5.13) above. To design a computer 'experiment' to illustrate the Heckscher-Ohlin theorem, the relative factor endowments must differ in the two countries. We present in Table 5.6 a computer program which assumes that the labour endowment is the same for each country: LA = LB = 2.0, but that the capital endowments differ: KA = 0.8, KB = 1.6. The program will be seen to be a simple adaptation of that in Table 5.3 with repetitive statements giving production and consumption relations and budget constraints for each country. (Space has been saved by noting that with the normalisation F = 1 for each country, the same domestic prices will be determined by world prices in each country, and the technical relations of production are assumed the same in both countries, so lines 100–180 define variables common to both.) The variables PW1 and PW2, exogenous in the model of Table 5.3, are now determined by an iteration procedure, using the equations (5.12) and (5.13).

It will be found that the values used for PW1 and PW2 in the one-country model lie near the equilibrium solution for the two-country model and the values PW1 = 1.4 and PW2 = 1.6 are suggested as INPUT values when the program is run.

Table 5.6 Computer Program for a Two-country Model

```
10 REM HECKSCHER-OHLIN TWO COUNTRY MODEL
20 REM SUGGESTED INPUT VALUES: PW1=1.4 AND PW2=1.6
30 LET KA = 0.8
40 LET KB = 1.6
50 LET LA = 2.0
60 LET LB = 1.8
70 LET F = 1
80 INPUT "INITIAL VALUE FOR PW1? "PW1
90 INPUT "INITIAL VALUE FOR PW2? "PW2
100 LET P1 = F*PW1
110 LET P2 = F*PW2
120 LET R = (P2^3*((1/3)^0.75+3^0.25)^2)/(8*P1^2)
130 LET W = (2*P1^2)/(P2*((1/3)^0.75+3^0.25)^2)
140 LET UK1 = (W/(3*R))^0.75
150 LET UK2 = (W/R)^0.5
160 LET UL1 = ((3*R)/W)^0.25
170 LET UL2 = (R/W)^0.5
180 LET A = UL1*UK2-UL2*UK1
190 LET X1A = (LA*UK2-KA*UL2)/A
200 LET X1B = (LB*UK2-KB*UL2)/A
210 LET X2A = (KA*UL1-LA*UK1)/A
220 LET X2B = (KB*UL1-LB*UK1)/A
230 LET K1A = UK1*X1A
240 LET K1B = UK1*X1B
250 LET K2A = UK2*X2A
260 LET K2B= UK2*X2B
270 LET L1A = UL1*X1A
280 LET L1B = UL1*X1B
290 LET L2A = UL2*X2A
300 LET L2B = UL2*X2B
310 LET YA = R*(K1A+K2A)+W*(L1A+L2A)
320 LET YB = R*(K1B+K2B)+W*(L1B+L2B)
330 LET C1A = YA/(2*P1)
340 LET C1B = YB/(2*P1)
350 LET C2A = YA/(2*P2)
360 LET C2B = YB/(2*P2)
370 LET MA = C2A-X2A
380 LET EB = X2B-C2B
390 LET EA = X1A-C1A
400 LET MB = C1B-X1B
```

```
410 LET BPA = (PW1*EA-PW2*MA)
420 LET BPB = (PW1*MB-PW2*EB)
430 IF ABS(EA-MB)<.01 AND  ABS(MA-EB)<0.01 THEN GOTO 520
440 IF EA>MB THEN LET PW1 = PW1-.001
450 IF EA<MB THEN LET PW1 = PW1+.001
460 PRINT "PW1 = "PW1
470 IF MA>EB THEN LET PW2 = PW2+.001
480 IF MA<EB THEN LET PW2 = PW2-.001
490 PRINT "PW2 = "PW2
500 PRINT
510 GOTO 100
520 PRINT
530 PRINT "EQUILIBRIUM PRICES"
540 PRINT "PW1 = "PW1
550 PRINT "PW2 = "PW2
560 PRINT "P1 = "P1
570 PRINT "P2 = "P2
580 PRINT "R = "R
590 PRINT "W = "W
600 PRINT "F = "F
610 PRINT
620 PRINT "DOMESTIC PRODUCTION"
630 PRINT "X1A = "X1A
640 PRINT "X1B =  "X1B
650 PRINT "X2A = "X2A
660 PRINT "X2B = "X2B
670 PRINT
680 PRINT "FOREIGN TRADE"
690 PRINT "EA = "EA
700 PRINT "MA = "MA
710 PRINT "EB = "EB
720 PRINT  "MB = "MB
730 PRINT "BPA=  "BPA
740 PRINT "BPB=  "BPB
```

This program (if it has been run successfully with BPA and BPB, the balance of payments variables, not significantly different from zero) should show that the relatively labour-abundant economy, Country A, exports good 1, the labour-intensive good, while Country B, better endowed with capital, exports the capital-intensive good 2.

The use of the above computer program does not, of course, tell us anything new about the Heckscher-Ohlin theorem, although it provides a striking visual illustration of the theorem. Further computer 'experiments' can, however, be used to explore a number of interesting issues. Experimenting with different values for the initial factor endowments and examining the consequences for the structure and level of world trade is one obvious use of the model. Comparisons between the 'autarchic' closed economy model solved by the computer program of Table 4.2 and the full two-country model solved by the program of Table 5.6 show the consequences of trade for all aspects of economic life: production, consumption, factor remuneration, the level of income. Some of these issues are explored further in Chapter 7, but first we introduce a new agent into the two-sector model — the government.

References

Bhagwati, J.N. and Srinivasan, T.N. (1983) *Lectures on International Trade*, MIT Press.
Sodersten, B. (1980) *International Economics* (2nd edn), Macmillan.

6

INTRODUCING THE PUBLIC SECTOR

6.1 Introduction

The two-sector general equilibrium models considered so far have assumed perfect competition in all the markets of the economy, and free trade in international markets. Such models are useful for illustrating the way in which the price mechanism works to allocate goods and services in a world of profit-maximising firms and utility-maximising consumers. Many interesting questions in economics, however, arise from situations in which the full set of assumptions for the perfectly competitive model is not satisfied. If, for example, there is a government which imposes taxes, the assumption of a single market clearing price no longer holds: with a tax on commodities, producers and consumers are faced by different prices in the same market; similarly, an import tariff means that there is a divergence between the world price of a commodity and the price paid by domestic consumers. What are the economic consequences of such divergencies? The two-sector model of this book can be used to consider questions of this kind, but in order to preserve the general equilibrium framework of the discussion, it is essential to show exactly how the government or the public sector (we shall use these terms interchangeably) can be incorporated into the structure of the model.

Two forms of public sector intervention in the economy are discussed in this chapter. In the first place, we consider the implications for the general equilibrium model of public sector production. To keep the discussion within the two-sector frame-work, it will be assumed that public sector production takes the form of producing either one of the two commodities of the model, or both; and that when the government engages in production it uses the two factors of production, capital and labour, so that the quantities of these factors available for private sector production are reduced. With these assumptions it is clear that public sector production will have consequences for both the commodity and the factor markets within the two-sector general equilibrium model. The second form of public sector intervention to be considered is the imposition of taxes. We shall consider three forms of taxation: lump-sum taxes, commodity taxes and tariffs, and in each case we shall show the consequences for the general equilibrium model of any market distortions created by the existence of taxation.

Central to the analysis of the role of the public sector in the two-sector model is the formulation of the public sector's budget constraint, and the perception that the government must balance its budget for a general equilibrium solution of the model. The introduction of the government into the model means that there is a new economic agent to be considered. When the government imposes taxes, or sells output produced within the public sector, it receives income; similarly, if it gives subsidies (which can be thought of as negative taxes) or employs factors of production, it incurs expenditures. For general equilibrium the public sector must satisfy its budget constraint with its income exactly equal to its expenditure. This means that the two areas of public sector intervention in the economy described in the last paragraph — public sector production and taxation — cannot always be considered independently If the public sector incurs production losses, these losses have to be counterbalanced by the imposition of taxes; similarly public sector profits must be redistributed to the consumer or the producers in the form of a subsidy.

In this chapter we develop an open-economy version of the two-sector model which includes public sector production and taxation; this model is then used in the following chapter to consider some of the interesting questions of public policy which arise when tax-distorted markets are incorporated in the general equilibrium model as a consequence of government activity.

6.2 Public Sector Production

When the government embarks on production in the two-sector model it adds to the supply of the two commodities. If we denote public sector production of goods 1 and 2 by G_1 and G_2 respectively, the commodity market clearing equations in the open economy model of the last chapter become

$$C_1 = X_1 + G_1 - E \qquad (6.1)$$
$$C_2 = X_2 + G_2 + M \qquad (6.2)$$

The factor market clearing equations, too, will be affected by the activities of the public sector as government production increases the demand for the two factors of production, capital and labour. If we denote the public sector use of these two factors by Kg and Lg, the factor market clearing equations become

$$K_1 + K_2 + Kg = K^\star \qquad (6.3)$$
$$L_1 + L_2 + Lg = L^\star \qquad (6.4)$$

How does the government make its production decisions? When private producers make their production decisions, they do so on a profit-maximising basis, taking into consideration the nature of their production functions and all the relative prices of the system. There are several ways in which the government's behaviour can be modelled. Public sector producers can be assumed to use the same technology as private sector producers, or a different one; public sector production decisions can be guided by profit-maximising principles, or they can be made along different lines. If the government's behaviour is indistinguishable from that of private sector producers, including public sector production in the two-sector model does not contribute a great deal to the analysis; in the exposition of this chapter we shall therefore assume that the public sector uses the same technology as the private firms, but that the government's decisions about levels of factor employment, and hence its output decisions are made independently. This implies that the new variables G_1, G_2, Kg and Lg introduced in equations (6.1) – (6.4) are to be treated as exogenous variables in the general equilibrium system.

Although levels of output and employment in the public sector are assumed to be exogenously determined, the activities of the public sector will have consequences for the general equilibrium system. By adding to the supply of goods 1 and 2, and by increasing the demand for factors of production, the government will influence the production and consumption decisions of the private sector. In a flexible price model, government intervention in the commodity and factor markets will affect all the relative prices of the system; in a fixed price model, such as the one considered in the last chapter, the full employment levels of output for the private sector, on which the general equilibrium solution depends, will be affected by the introduction of Kg and Lg in the factor market clearing equations (6.3) and (6.4). In both cases the general equilibrium solution of the model will be altered by the inclusion of public sector production.

A further way in which public sector production decisions are interwoven with the rest of the economic system comes from adopting the assumption that although the quantities of the goods produced in the public sector are exogenously determined, the government does not exercise direct control over the prices of the general equilibrium system. It employs its factors at the market rental and wage rates, and it sells its output at the market prices. Government income from public sector production, which we denote by G, is therefore described, assuming both goods are produced in the public sector, by

$$G = P_1 G_1 + P_2 G_2 - rKg - wLg \qquad (6.5)$$

G depends upon the relative prices of the general equilibrium system, as well as upon the exogenous variables G_1, G_2, Kg and Lg, and is therefore an endogenous variable of the model. G represents the income of the government from public sector production, and for the general equilibrium system including government to be fully formulated, it is necessary to consider how this government income is to be incorporated in the model.

It is an essential assumption for a real general equilibrium model that the government must balance its budget, with its income exactly equal to its expenditures. If there were a budget surplus or deficit, this would imply that one of the other budget constraints in the model, or one of the market clearing equations, was not satisfied; and this would contravene the principles upon which a model of general equilibrium is constructed. We explore this issue further in the next chapter when we discuss the relation between the public sector budget constraint and the balance of payments. Meanwhile, we assume that government income from production, G in the model, must be exactly matched by an equal inflow or outflow of funds so that the government's net income is equal to zero. If public sector production makes a profit, so that G is a positive quantity, this income must be transferred to the private sector as a subsidy; if public sector production makes a loss, and G is negative, taxes must be imposed to raise the necessary revenue needed to balance the public sector budget.

6.3 Balancing the Public Sector Budget: Taxes and Subsidies in the General Equilibrium Model

The condition that the government must balance its budget can be represented by the equation

$$G + T = 0 \tag{6.6}$$

where the variable T represents the net revenues of the public sector from taxes and subsidies. We discuss in this section some of the ways in which the government can raise revenues in the two-sector general equilibrium model. Lump-sum taxes, commodity taxes and tariffs will first be considered as separate mechanisms for balancing the public sector budget; later in the chapter we shall consider a model which includes all these taxes. In each case, the analysis will be equally applicable for a tax or a subsidy. For example, a lump-sum tax on the consumer's income will reduce his income by a given amount; a lump-sum subsidy of the same absolute size will increase the consumer's income by the same amount. From an analytic point of view a subsidy can be treated as a negative tax, so the following discussion will be conducted in terms of tax revenues only; the effects of subsidies can be modelled by assuming that the tax variables have a negative sign.

Assuming that public sector production is running at a loss, taxes have to be imposed. The simplest tax to consider, and one that has a certain theoretical interest, is a lump-sum tax on the consumer's income. If we represent the lump-sum tax by t_Y, the consumer's income in the two-sector model will be given by

$$Y = rK^\star + wL^\star - t_Y \tag{6.7}$$

where $K^\star$ and $L^\star$ are defined by (6.3) and (6.4) above. The level of the lump-sum tax will be determined by

$$t_Y = T \tag{6.8}$$

where T is, from (6.6), equal to the public sector production losses.

The reason why lump-sum taxes are of interest to economic theorists is that the imposition of a lump sum tax does not in itself change any of the relative prices of the model. The consumer has less income to dispose of, but the prices of the factor services he has to offer, and the prices of the commodities he can buy, are unaffected by the tax, and the imposition of the tax will not lead him to substitute one good for another in his expenditure decisions.

For this reason, lump-sum taxes are often described as 'non-distortionary', and contrasted with other 'distortionary' taxes which change relative prices. In this model the tax t_Y is referred to as a lump-sum tax although it could in the present context equally well be described as an income tax. The reason for preferring the term 'lump-sum tax' is that in the real world income taxes may have distortionary effects if they lead individuals to substitute leisure for work or vice versa. In the two-sector general equilibrium model developed in this text full employment is assumed throughout, and the quantities of capital and labour supplied do not vary, so that the terms 'income tax' and 'lump-sum tax' can be used synonymously.

We now consider how a commodity tax can be introduced into the general equilibrium system. Either good could be taxed; we will assume that the government decides to finance its deficit by imposing a tax on the consumption of good 1. This tax, which we denote by t_C, will have the effect of driving a wedge between the consumer and the producer price for good 1. Two different variables will have to be used in the model to represent the consumer price and the producer price. Using Q_1, to denote the producer price, and retaining P_1 for the producer price, we have

$$Q_1 - P_1 + t_C \qquad (6.9)$$

The government will collect a sum equal to t_C for each unit of good 1 purchased by the consumer, so the total tax revenue received by the government will be given by

$$T = t_C C_1 \qquad (6.10)$$

In order to determine the level at which t_C should be set we can rearrange this equation to read

$$t_C = \frac{T}{C_1} \qquad (6.10a)$$

where T is determined from the equation necessary to balance the public sector budget, equation (6.6) above.

The last tax we consider in this section is a trade tax. Governments frequently impose import tariffs for reasons other than the need to balance the public sector budget, and typically the level of such a tariff in the real world is fixed by the desired level of protection for the domestic producers of the good in question. Later models in this book will assume a fixed import tariff, but here we show how in principle the level of the tariff could be determined endogenously to meet the public sector budget constraint. An import tariff, t_M will be levied on imported goods only. The consequence of this form of taxation is to introduce a distortion between the world price of the imported good and its domestic price. Using the notation of previous chapters, and assuming that as in the model of the previous chapter, good 2 is the imported good, we have[1]

$$P_2 = FP_{W2} + t_M \qquad (6.11)$$

Total tax revenues will now depend upon the level of imports

$$T = t_M M \qquad (6.12)$$

and the level of t_M required to satisfy the public sector budget constraint (6.6) can be found by solving (6.12)

$$t_M = \frac{T}{M} \qquad (6.12a)$$

where once again the desired level of T is determined by the extent of the production losses in the public sector.

We are now in a position where we can formulate a two-sector general equilibrium model including both public sector production and the tax revenue from any one of the three taxes considered above. Depending upon the tax adjustment mechanism chosen, an open economy model incorporating either constant returns or decreasing returns to scale, will include the new endogenous variables G, T (determined by the public sector budget constraint), and either t_Y, t_C or t_M. In the case of the commodity tax the consumer price Q_1 would also be a new endogenous variable in the model. As explained in Section 6.2, the new variables G_1, G_2, Kg and Lg are assumed to be exogenous. The model including a public sector will have to add as many new equations as there are new endogenous variables. The additional equations will be (6.5) to define G; (6.6) to define T; and either (6.8), (6.10a) or (6.12a) to define the tax chosen to balance the budget. With the commodity tax adjustment mechanism, the equation (6.9) will also be included to define the variable Q_1. Other changes required for all three

---

1. Per unit taxes have been assumed for the commodity tax and the import tax. With proportional taxes the relations of (6.9) and (6.11) would become $Q_1 = P_1(1 + t_C)$ and $P_2 = FP_{W2}(1 + t_M)$.

versions of the model will be the adaptation of the market clearing equations which will now be described by equations (6.1) – (6.4). With the commodity tax adjustment mechanism, the price of good 1 entering the consumer's demand function will be Q_1, not P_1; and with the import tariff adjustment mechanism, the equation (6.11) will replace the equation describing the relation between the world price of good 2 and its domestic price under free trade.

Rather than setting out the full set of equations for these three essentially repetitive models, we present in the next section a model which includes public sector production, and all three taxes discussed above. In this model, total tax revenues will equal the sum of the tax receipts from each of the separate taxes:

$$T = t_Y + t_C C_1 + t_M M \qquad (6.13)$$

The satisfaction of the public sector budget constraint (6.6) requires that the income from all three taxes taken together should equal any production losses incurred. The implications of this for the exogeneity or endogeneity of the individual tax rates are discussed in the following section after the presentation of the model equations in Table 6.1.

6.4 Equations for a Model Including Government

The model presented in this section includes public sector production, a lump-sum tax, a commodity tax, and an import tariff. It is, of course, only one of the large number of models that could be constructed within the two-sector framework which would include public sector as well as private sector activity. It should, in common with the other models in this book, be viewed as representative, rather than in any way definitive. To keep the model reasonably simple we assume that the government produces only one of the two goods, good 2, and that one commodity tax and one trade tax are imposed. (If desired, the reader could interpret the model in terms of an import substitution policy: the public sector adds to the domestic production of the imported good which is protected by the imposition of an import tariff; domestic consumption of the export good is discouraged by a commodity tax.) The model of Table 6.1 is based on the open economy model of the previous chapter (set out in Table 5.1), and therefore exhibits constant returns to scale. The reader could easily enlarge the model to include public sector production of good 1, a second commodity tax, or an export subsidy; and the construction of a decreasing returns to scale model including government would proceed on identical lines to the present model.

The modifications necessary to integrate the public sector into the open economy model of Table 5.1 are as follows. Public sector production will be included in the model by substituting (6.2) – (6.4) for the corresponding market clearing equations, and by adding (6.5) (without the term in G_1) to define the government's income from production. The inclusion of a commodity tax and an import tariff imply the addition of the price equation (6.9) to distinguish between the consumer and the producer price of good 1, and the substitution of (6.11) for the existing equation defining the relation between the world price and the domestic price of good 2. The public sector budget constraint will be incorporated in the model by adding (6.6) and total tax revenues will be defined by equation (6.13).

At this stage the model will consist of 24 equations — the original 20 equations of Table 5.1 (modified where necessary) plus (6,5), (6,6), (6.9) and (6.13). What are the endogenous variables of the model? There are the 20 variables listed at the end of Table 5.1 and repeated here for convenience: C_1 C_2 X_1 X_2 K_1 K_2 L_1 L_2 k_1 k_2 l_1 l_2 P_1 P_2 w r Y E M and F; and there are the new variables G T and Q_1. This makes a total of 23 variables in all. Three more variables remain to be considered; these are the three taxes t_Y, t_C and t_M. How are the values of these taxes to be determined within the model? Twenty-four equations will not be enough to determine the values of a total of 26 variables. One solution to this problem, and the one we adopt for the model of this chapter, is to assume that two of the tax levels are determined exogenously, and the third is determined endogenously to satisfy the public sector budget constraint. A more sophisticated solution to the problem would be to use mathematical optimising techniques to choose the optimal set of values for the taxes. This would provide further equations for the model which would enable the system to be 'closed' with the same number of equations as endogenous variables. The theory of optimal taxation, however, is too advanced to be considered in this book, and for our present model we fall back on the simple expedient of assuming one endogenous and two exogenous taxes. The choice of tax to be endogenous does not affect the equations of the model which we present in Table 6.1, and we arbitrarily include the lump-sum tax t_Y in the list of endogenous variables and assume the commodity tax and import tariff are fixed tax rates, set exogenously by the government. The numerical example of the following section explores alternative assumptions.

Table 6.1 An Open Economy Model Including Government

COMMODITY MARKETS

Demand	$C_1 = C_1(Q_1, P_2 Y)$	(1)
	$C_2 = C_2(Q_1, P_2, Y)$	(2)
Unit price equations	$P_1 = rk_1 + wl_1$	(3)
	$P_2 = rk_2 + wl_2$	(4)
Market clearing	$C_1 = X_1 - E$	(5)
	$C_2 = X_2 + G_2 + M$	(6)
Price equation	$Q_1 = P_1 + t_C$	(7)

FACTOR MARKETS

Private sector demand	$k_1 = k_1(r, w)$	(8)
	$K_1 = k_1 X_1$	(9)
	$k_2 = k_2(r, w)$	(10)
	$K_2 = k_2 X_2$	(11)
	$l_1 = l_1(r, w)$	(12)
	$L_1 = l_1 X_1$	(13)
	$l_2 = l_2(r, w)$	(14)
	$L_2 = l_2 X_2$	(15)
Market clearing	$K_1 + K_2 + Kg = K^\star$	(16)
	$L_1 + L_2 + Lg = L^\star$	(17)

CONSUMER'S INCOME

	$Y = rK^\star + wL^\star - t_Y$	(18)

PUBLIC SECTOR

Income from production	$G = P_2 G_2 - rKg - wLg$	(19)
Tax revenue	$T = t_Y + t_C C_1 + t_M M$	(20)
Budget constraint	$G + T = 0$	(21)

FOREIGN SECTOR

Price equations	$P_1 = FP_{W1}$	(22)
	$P_2 = FP_{W2} + t_M$	(23)
Balance of payments constraint	$P_{W1}E - P_{W2}M = 0$	(24)

The 24 endogenous variables are C_1 C_2 X_1 X_2 K_1 K_2 L_1 L_2 k_1 k_2 l_1 l_2 P_1 Q_1 P_2 w r Y E M F G T t_Y

The variables $K^\star$ $L^\star$ P_{W1} P_{W2} G_2 Kg Lg t_C t_M are exogenous.

6.5   A Numerical Example

A specific numerical example of the model of Table 6.1 is included in this chapter, not only to demonstrate how the solution of the general equilibrium model varies, depending upon which tax is assumed to be endogenous, but also to present a comprehensive model which will be used to illustrate a number of propositions in economic theory in the next chapter.

We shall continue to assume the same production and consumption relations for the private sector as in the open economy model of Chapter 5. Substituting these relations in the general model of Table 6.1 gives the specific example in Table 6.2.

Table 6.2 A Numerical Example of an Open Economy Model Including Government

---

COMMODITY MARKETS

Demand

$$C_1 = \frac{Y}{2Q_1} \tag{1}$$

$$C_2 = \frac{Y}{2P_2} \tag{2}$$

Unit price equations

$$P_1 = rk_1 + wl_1 \tag{3}$$
$$P_2 = rk_2 + wl_2 \tag{4}$$

Market clearing

$$C_1 = X_1 - E \tag{5}$$
$$C_2 = X_2 + G_2 + M \tag{6}$$

Price equation

$$Q_1 = P_1 + t_C \tag{7}$$

FACTOR MARKETS

Private sector demand

$$k_1 = \left(\frac{w}{3r}\right)^{\frac{3}{4}} \tag{8}$$

$$K_1 = k_1 X_1 \tag{9}$$

$$k_2 = \left(\frac{w}{r}\right)^{\frac{1}{2}} \tag{10}$$

$$K_2 = k_2 X_2 \tag{11}$$

$$l_1 = \left(\frac{3r}{w}\right)^{\frac{1}{4}} \tag{12}$$

$$L_1 = l_1 X_1 \tag{13}$$

$$l_2 = \left(\frac{r}{w}\right)^{\frac{1}{2}} \tag{14}$$

$$L_2 = l_2 X_2 \tag{15}$$

Market clearing
$$K_1 + K_2 + Kg = K^\star \tag{16}$$
$$L_1 + L_2 + Lg = L^\star \tag{17}$$

CONSUMER'S INCOME

$$Y = rK^\star + wL^\star - t_Y \tag{18}$$

PUBLIC SECTOR

Income from production
$$G = P_2 G_2 - rKg - wLg \tag{19}$$

Tax revenue
$$T = t_Y + t_C C_1 + t_M M \tag{20}$$

Budget constraint
$$G + T = 0 \tag{21}$$

FOREIGN SECTOR

Price equations
$$P_1 = F(P_{W1}) \tag{22}$$
$$P_2 = F(P_{W2}) + t_M \tag{23}$$

Balance of payments
constraint
$$P_{W1} E - P_{W2} M = 0 \tag{24}$$

The 24 endogenous variables are C_1 C_2 X_1 X_2 K_1 K_2 L_1 L_2 k_1 k_2 l_1 l_2 P_1 Q_1 P_2 w r Y E M F G T and EITHER t_Y OR t_C

The variables $K^\star$ $L^\star$ P_{W1} P_{W2} G_2 Kg Lg t_M and EITHER t_Y OR t_C are exogenous.

It will be observed in Table 6.2 that in the list of endogenous and exogenous variables t_Y and t_C have been included as alternatives so that the consequences of using each of the adjustment mechanism can be explored using the computer program of Table 6.3. The import tariff t_M is assumed fixed throughout, but it would be a trivial extension of the program to allow this variable, too, to be considered as the endogenous variable used to balance the public sector budget.

The only problem remaining before writing a computer program to solve the model of Table 6.2 is to assign values to the exogenous variables and the exogenous relations of the model. We maintain continuity with the earlier numerical examples by retaining the same values for the initial factor endowments and the world prices: $K^\star = 0.8$, $L^\star = 2.0$, $P_{W1} = 1.4$, $P_{W2} = 1.6$. Values now have to be assigned to the exogenous public sector variables. Given the assumption that, unlike the private sector, the government is not guided by profit-maximising principles when making its employment decisions, the values of Kg and Lg can be assigned arbitrarily. We assume the values $Kg = 0.1$ and $Lg = 0.2$. What assumption should be made about the technology adopted by the public sector in its production of good 2? As noted earlier, any assumption can be made; we assume for the purposes of this example that the government production function is the same as that of firm 2, so

$$G_2 = Kg^{1/2}Lg^{1/2} \tag{6.14}$$

Values also have to be assigned to the exogenous tax variables, t_M and either t_Y or t_C. Rather than writing two programs, one with t_C exogenous and t_Y endogenous, and one with t_Y exogenous and t_C endogenous, the program of Table 6.3 is designed to allow the user to choose between t_Y and t_C (TY and TC in the program) as adjustment mechanisms. All three taxes are initially set equal to zero and the program uses an iterative procedure to find the value of the endogenous tax which just balances the public sector budget. This variable is given the name PSB in the computer program of Table 6.3, and is defined at line 420:

420 LET PSB = G + T

where, as in the text, G is the public sector's income from production, defined at line 400 from equation (19) in the model of Table 6.2, and T is the total tax revenue, defined at line 410 from model equation (20). In order to satisfy the government's budget constraint (equation (21) in the model of Table 6.2) it is necessary to have

$$PSB = 0 \tag{6.15}$$

and this condition provides the basis for the alternative iteration procedures in lines 430 – 520.

The only other new variables used in this program are KX and LX which represent the quantities of capital and labour available for use by the private sector after the requirements of the public sector have been met. The values of these variables, defined at lines 260 and 270, are determined from the factor market clearing equations, (16) and (17) in the model. These residual quantities provide the basis for the full employment conditions in the open economy, and the analysis of production (and consumption) in this model is identical to that of the previous chapter. It will be noted that although the program in Table 6.3, including the public sector in the model, is longer than previous ones, it need only take a few minutes to write, as it is a straightforward adaptation of the open economy program of Table 5.3.

Table 6.3 Computer Program for the Model including Government

```
 10 REM OPEN ECONOMY MODEL WITH PUBLIC SECTOR
 20 PRINT "CHOOSE TAX ADJUSTMENT MECHANISM:"
 30 PRINT "TY FOR LUMPSUM TAX; TC FOR COMMODITY TAX"
 40 INPUT "WHICH TAX? " TAX$
 50 LET K = 0.8
 60 LET L= 2.0
 70 LET KG = 0.1
 80 LET LG = 0.2
 90 LET G2 =   KG^0.5*LG^0.5
100 LET TY = 0
110 LET TC = 0
120 LET TM = 0
130 LET PW1 = 1.4
140 LET PW2 = 1.6
150 LET F = 1
160 LET P1 = F*PW1
170 LET Q1 = P1+TC
180 LET P2 = F*PW2+TM
190 LET R = (P2^3*((1/3)^0.75+3^0.25)^2)/(8*P1^2)
200 LET W = (2*P1^2)/(P2*((1/3)^0.75+3^0.25)^2)
210 LET UK1 = (W/(3*R))^0.75
220 LET UK2 = (W/R)^0.5
230 LET UL1 = ((3*R)/W)^0.25
240 LET UL2 = (R/W)^0.5
250 LET A = UL1*UK2-UL2*UK1
260 LET KX = K-KG
270 LET LX = L-LG
280 LET X1 = (LX*UK2-KX*UL2)/A
290 LET X2 = (KX*UL1-LX*UK1)/A
300 LET K1 = UK1*X1
310 LET K2 = UK2*X2
320 LET L1 = UL1*X1
330 LET L2 = UL2*X2
340 LET Y = R*K+W*L-TY
350 LET C1 = Y/(2*Q1)
```

```
360 LET C2 = Y/(2*P2)
370 LET M = C2-X2-G2
380 LET E = X1-C1
390 LET BP = (PW1*E-PW2*M)
400 LET G = P2*G2-R*KG-W*LG
410 LET T = TY+TC*C1+TM*M
420 LET PSB = G+T
430 IF ABS(PSB)<0.001 THEN GOTO 530
440 IF TAX$ = "TY" AND PSB>0 THEN LET TY = TY-0.001
450 IF TAX$ = "TY" AND PSB<0 THEN LET TY = TY+0.001
460 IF TAX$ = "TC" AND PSB>0 THEN LET TC = TC-0.001
470 IF TAX$ = "TC" AND PSB<0 THEN LET TC = TC+0.001
480 PRINT "PSB = "PSB
490 PRINT "TY = "TY
500 PRINT "TC = "TC
510 PRINT
520 GOTO 170
530 PRINT
540 PRINT "EQUILIBRIUM PRICES"
550 PRINT "P1 = "P1
560 PRINT "Q1 = "Q1
570 PRINT "P2 = "P2
580 PRINT "R = "R
590 PRINT "W = "W
600 PRINT "F = "F
610 PRINT
620 PRINT "PRIVATE SECTOR OUTPUT AND EMPLOYMENT"
630 PRINT "X1 = "X1
640 PRINT "X2 = "X2
650 PRINT "K1 = "K1
660 PRINT "K2 = "K2
670 PRINT "L1 = "L1
680 PRINT "L2 = "L2
690 PRINT
700 PRINT "PUBLIC SECTOR"
710 PRINT "G2 = "G2
720 PRINT "G = "G
730 PRINT "T = "T
740 PRINT "PSB = "PSB
750 PRINT "TC = "TC
760 PRINT "TY = "TY
770 PRINT
780 PRINT "FOREIGN SECTOR"
790 PRINT "E = "E
800 PRINT "M = "M
810 PRINT "BP= "BP
```

When the program is run, it will be seen that, with the specific assumptions made about the employment levels and the technology used to produce good 2 in the public sector, government production operates at a loss, and taxes have to be imposed to balance the budget (with different assumptions the public sector could make a profit, and subsidies would be seen to result from running the program.) As in the earlier open economy program, the final equilibrium should show, from Walras' Law, that the balance of payments is insignificantly different from zero.

We do not give the numerical values resulting from running the computer program in Table 6.3 because the program is deliberately written to provide the basis for many different experiments each leading to a different solution. In the solution to the program as written in Table 6.3 there will be only one non-zero tax rate, as discussed in the analysis of Section 6.3. Users can experiment with different values for the tax rates chosen to be exogenous in the model; for example, values of 0.05, or 0.1, would provide appropriate rates to experiment with, and could be written into the program at lines 100 – 120. The next chapter uses a number of such experiments to consider some familiar propositions from economic theory.

7

TRADE THEORY AND THE TWO-SECTOR MODEL

7.1 Introduction

The basic two-sector closed economy model of the first few chapters of this book has now been extended to include both international trade and a public sector. Of the usual extensions to the circular flow diagram of Figure 1.1 only savings and investment are excluded as these issues would require an intertemporal model for a satisfactory treatment. In this chapter we make use of the models and the numerical examples of Chapters 1 – 6 to illustrate some propositions from the theory of international trade. Two important theorems — the Rybczynski theorem and the Heckscher-Ohlin-Samuelson theorem — were illustrated at the end of Chapter 5 in the course of the discussion about the role of factor endowments in the open economy. This chapter uses numerical examples to examine the potential gains from trade, the effects of a protective tariff, the Stolper-Samuelson theorem, the general equilibrium implications of a monopolistic export market, and the link between the public sector budget and the balance of payments. For most of these illustrations we confine ourselves to the various versions of the one-consumer, two-good, two-factor model of earlier chapters, but, where relevant, we show how the reader who wishes to extend the numerical examples to examine some of the above issues in a two-country framework can build the analysis into the two-country model presented at the end of Chapter 5. Some of the problems that arise and the distributive issues that can be discussed when more than one consumer is included in the model are considered at the end of this chapter in Section 7.7.

The coverage of trade issues is necessarily selective and the analysis is not intended to teach students the theory of international trade; the suggested exercises are activities that can usefully complement the more orthodox textbook approach. The use of specific models which can be solved by the computer solution procedures presented in the text has the advantage that it enables the full general equilibrium consequences of any change in assumption to be perceived. Equally important, the use of computers which can do calculations in seconds makes it possible to experiment with the models, and to see which of the conclusions that may be drawn from the specific examples are sensitive to changes in the parameters of the model, or changes in its basic structure. We shall discuss only a few of the many possible 'experiments', but it is hoped that the reader who is interested in this approach to learning economics will be encouraged to explore a wider range of subjects.

The computer-user who wishes to try the experiments described in this chapter will find line by line instructions for adapting the earlier models and programs. The models and programs are not listed in full in this chapter because in most cases only minor modifications to models given earlier are required to illustrate the theorems considered.

7.2   The Measurement of Changes in Welfare

A problem that has to be confronted in the analysis of this chapter is that many of the propositions from the theory of international trade are concerned with questions of welfare. In order to be able to use general equilibrium models to discuss normative as well as positive issues in trade theory, a measure of economic welfare is required. The definition of welfare and the measurement of welfare change are major subjects that pose many problems for the applied economist. Three interrelated questions are involved: firstly, what does economic welfare depend upon? secondly, how can changes in an individual's economic welfare be measured? and thirdly, how can the welfare consequences of an economic change which affects different individuals in different ways be assessed?

In the formal one-consumer models developed in this book, a simple definition of economic welfare has in fact been implicit in the way in which the consumer's behaviour has been modelled. The demand functions have been derived from the assumption that the consumer maximises utility, and utility has been defined in terms of the quantities of the two commodities consumed. The general utility function was described in Chapter 1 by the relation

$$U = U(C_1, C_2) \tag{7.1}$$

and the specific form introduced in Chapter 2 and used in all the subsequent numerical examples as the function underlying the demand relationships was

$$U = C_1^{1/2} C_2^{1/2} \tag{7.2}$$

This suggests that an appropriate measure of welfare change for the one-consumer, two-good economy model would be changes in the levelof U. Accordingly, we use this measure in the trade theory analysis of the present chapter: an increase in the value of U is taken to imply an improvement in social welfare; a decrease in the value of U is taken to imply a loss of welfare. It is important to emphasise that the actual numerical values of the variable U have no particular significance. It is not being asserted that changes in U provide a cardinal measure of welfare change in terms of 'utils'; U is to be regarded as an ordinal measure of utility, with changes in the level of U providing a measure of the direction of welfare change.[1] Any monotonic transformation of the utility function would serve equally well as a basis for measuring changes in the level of welfare. The possibility of obtaining cardinal measures of welfare change from ordinal ones is an important question in welfare economics, but it is not discussed here.[2]

In order to find the value of the utility function in the computer programs written to solve any of the numerical examples of general equilibrium models introduced so far, the following two lines can be added:

900 LET U = C1^0.5*C2^0.5
910 PRINT "INDEX OF WELFARE (U) "U

For several of the computer experiments described in this chapter we shall report changes in the value of U, as well as changes in the values of relative prices and the real variables of the model.

---

1. Strictly speaking, the utility function should be defined as $U = U(C_1, C_2, K^\star, L^\star)$ since the consumer's welfare must be assumed to depend upon factor services supplied as well as on commodities consumed. However, as $K^\star$ and $L^\star$ have been assumed fixed at their full employment levels, with $dK^\star = dL^\star = 0$, changes in the level of utility will depend only on changes in the levels of consumption, so (7.1) provides an adequate basis for the measurement of welfare change.
2. Readers wishing to pursue this subject could look at any of the following books, listed in order of ascending difficulty: Mishan (1981), Boadway and Bruce (1984), McKenzie (1983).

The last of the three problems involved in the measurement of welfare change in an economy listed above, the problem of weighing up the social value of gains and losses accruing to different individuals, cannot arise in the two-sector models considered so far in this book, because we have throughout made the simplifying assumption that there is only one consumer. With only one consumer, who is assumed to receive all the income from factor employment and any profits made in either the private or the public sector, questions of distribution do not arise. Once there are two or more consumers with differing ownership of the initial factor endowments, and/or with differing utility functions, economic change will clearly have different consequences for the different individuals in the economy. If in a two-consumer economy both individuals gain, or both lose, the direction of the change in social welfare will be unambiguously determined. If, however, one gains and the other loses, the calculation of welfare change will not be possible without an explicit value judgement about the relative importance of the change in the utility of each. One way of formalising this value judgement is to use a social welfare function, often referred to as a Bergson-Samuelson welfare function. With two consumers, A and B, the social welfare function W would be a function of the utility of each:

$$W = W(U_A, U_B)$$

Without such a relation, however, it is difficult to draw any conclusions about the welfare consequences of an economic change which leads to gains for some, and losses for others.

The way in which a two-person economy can be modelled is discussed briefly in the last section of this chapter, but for the discussion of trade theory in Sections 7.3 – 7.6 we continue to assume that there is only one consumer. The single consumer is assumed to be representative of society as a whole, so that changes in the level of his or her utility can be identified with changes in the overall level of social welfare. This convention is commonly used by economists wishing to abstract from questions of distribution in order to concentrate upon problems dealing with the allocation of resources.

7.3   The Gains from Trade

For our first illustration of trade theory using the general equilibrium models of this text we consider a demonstration of the gains from trade. The nature of the potential gains from trade was discussed with the use of diagrams at the beginning of Chapter 5. It was shown there that if the world price ratio differed from the price ratio prevailing in the 'autarchic' economy, producers would be led to increase the production of the good in which the economy had a comparative advantage, and the consumer would be able to move to a higher indifference curve. Figure 5.3, repeated here as Figure 7.1, shows that in the closed economy production and consumption are both at point Q; in the open economy, production is at the point R and the consumer moves to the point T which lies on a higher indifference curve than the initial point Q. The gaps between production and consumption are met by importing good 2, and exporting good 1.

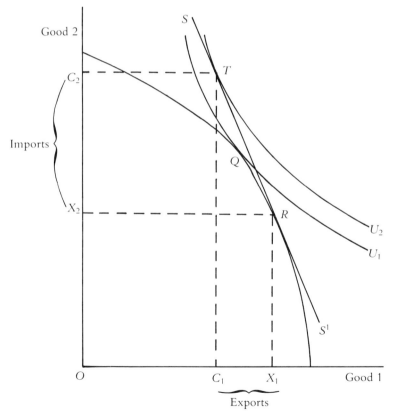

Figure 7.1 The Gains from Trade

This analysis can be extended by means of a simple computer experiment. The same assumptions underlie the relations of production and consumption in the numerical examples for the closed economy model of Chapter 4, and the open economy model of Chapter 5. By running the two computer programs given in Table 4.2 and Table 5.3 we can see the consequences of opening the economy to world trade at fixed world prices. The resulting equilibrium values for the real variables, the relative prices, and the welfare index U for the pre-trade and the post-trade economies are given in Table 7.1.

Table 7.1 Numerical Illustrations of the Gains from Trade

The Closed Economy	The Open Economy
$C1 = 0.82$	$C1 = 0.80$
$C2 = 0.65$	$C2 = 0.70$
$X1 = 0.82$	$X1 = 1.35$
$X2 = 0.65$	$X2 = 0.21$
$K1 = 0.26$	$K1 = 0.59$
$K2 = 0.53$	$K2 = 0.21$
$L1 = 1.20$	$L1 = 1.79$
$L2 = 0.80$	$L2 = 0.21$
$E = 0$	$E = 0.56$
$M = 0$	$M = 0.49$
$P1 = 1$	$P1 = 1$
$P2/P1 = 1.26$	$P2/P1 = 1.14$
$R/P1 = 0.78$	$R/P1 = 0.57$
$W/P1 = 0.51$	$W/P1 = 0.57$
$U = 0.73$	$U = 0.75$

Note: The computer programs of Table 4.2 and 5.3 were written using different numeraires. The relative prices for each equilibrium solution have therefore been recalculated in terms of a common numeraire, good 1, by calculating each price relative to P1.

The numerical results of Table 7.1 confirm the earlier diagrammatic analysis. With the opening up of the economy to trade the relative price of the two commodities changes: production of good

1 increases and production of good 2 decreases; the household adjusts its consumption pattern to take advantage of the new set of relative prices, consuming more of good 2 and slightly less of good 1; the resulting domestic shortfall of good 2 is met by imports, which are paid for by exporting part of the extra production of good 1. The index of social welfare U has increased in value, showing that the consumer has moved to a preferred position on his or her indifference map.

What additional information can be gleaned from the computer experiment which is not already evident from the diagram of Figure 7.1? One advantage of the numerical example is that it enables us to link the analysis of changes in production in the commodity markets to a discussion of factor-intensity and changes in relative prices in the factor markets. As noted in Section 5.4, the particular production functions used for the constant returns to scale model imply that industry 1 is relatively labour-intensive, and industry 2 is relatively capital-intensive. (This statement can be confirmed by calculating the equilibrium capital/labour ratios for each firm from Table 7.1.) With the change in relative prices caused by the introduction of world trade, production of the labour-intensive good becomes relatively more profitable. The figures of Table 7.1 show that as both capital and labour resources are shifted from the production of good 2 to the production of good 1, the price of labour rises and the relative price of capital falls. This observation is of comparatively little significance in a one-consumer model, but, as we discuss below in the context of the Stolper-Samuelson theorem, changes in relative factor prices are of great importance in models with more than one consumer and an unequal ownership of the factors of production.

It is not of course necessary to use a numerical general equilibrium model to discuss implications of trade for the factor markets as well as the commodity markets; questions of factor intensity and relative factor prices can be discussed by drawing further diagrams to illustrate different aspects of the two-sector model. The advantage of the specific numerical example is that it provides a unified treatment of the important interrelationships underlying the analysis of the gains from trade. Models of this kind have the further advantage, stressed in the introduction to this chapter, that alternative numerical examples can very easily be constructed, which means that the generality of the results derived above can be tested. (A simple experiment would be to write an open economy version of the decreasing returns to scale model of Chapter 2, and, by comparing the solution of the 'autarchic' model with the solution of the open economy model, to see which of the above conclusions are confirmed without the assumption of constant returns to scale.) Chapter 5 has already shown how different patterns of production and consumption will result from the introduction of trade, depending upon the assumptions made about initial factor endowments, and the world prices faced by the economy. It was shown there that by experimenting with different values for these variables, general equilibrium solutions can result with good 1 or good 2 as the importable or the exportable, and with domestic production of both goods or with specialisation in the production of one good only.

How can the models of our book contribute to an understanding of the origins of world trade which underlie the potential gains discussed in this section? The explanation of the gains from trade is usually presented in terms of comparative advantage. A country is said to have a comparative advantage in the production of one of two goods if in the pre-trade situation its relative cost of production is less than that prevailing abroad. In the pre-trade economy of our numerical example the autarchic price ratio will be equal to the relative marginal costs of the profit-maximising firms; the ratio of P_1 to P_2, $1/1.26$, shows that one unit of good 1 exchanges for 0.79 units of good 2, while the rate of exchange abroad reflected in the world price ratio ($P_{W1}/P_{W2} = 1.4/1.6$) is one unit of X_1 for 0.88 units of X_2. In the post-trade situation domestic resources have been reallocated so that relative production costs and relative domestic prices are equated with the world price ratios, with the consequences already discussed. To explain the origins of the gains from trade it is necessary to explain why autarchic price ratios may be supposed to diverge from world price ratios so that there are differences in comparative costs. Two possible reasons for the divergence between domestic price ratios and world price ratios are identified by trade theorists. One is differences in factor abundance between countries with similar technologies; the other is the existence of different technologies in different economies.

Exploration of the origins of trade patterns requires a two-country model, and the first of the above two explanations for differences in comparative advantage has already been illustrated in Chapter 5 by means of the Heckscher-Ohlin-Samuelson model of Section 5.5. This framework could also be used to explore the other explanation for the basis for differences in comparative advantage. By altering the assumptions made about the production functions and deriving the new factor demand relations (using the mathematical procedures of Chapter 2) new equilibrium solutions could be obtained and again the pre-trade and the post-trade situations of each country could be compared. By adding statements to the computer program of Table 5.6 defining variables UA and UB along the lines suggested in the previous section to measure the utility of the consumers in each country, and then comparing the pre-trade and the post-trade equilibrium values of UA and UB, a further dimension to the gains from trade could be explored: the distribution of gains between countries. We leave these further computer experiments for the reader, and return to an important aspect of the discussion of the gains from trade which has so far been omitted.

The results of the computer experiment reported in Table 7.1 show unambiguously that in the one-consumer economy the introduction of world trade leads to an increase in social welfare. This does not imply that in a many-consumer economy all will benefit from trade. On the contrary, it is likely, as with many policy changes, that some will be better off and some will be worse off. It can be demonstrated that free trade accompanied by appropriate tax changes to redistribute income from the gainers to the losers will be Pareto-superior to autarchy. This means that there is a potential gain from trade in the sense that it is possible for at least one person to be better off and none to be worse off. However, without the assurance that the appropriate tax changes will be made, the assertion that international trade will raise the level of welfare can only be made with certainty in a one-consumer economy. This question is taken up in the discussion of the Stolper-Samuelson theorem in the next section.

7.4 The Effects of Protection and the Stolper–Samuelson Theorem

The effects of protection in the two-sector model can be modelled by considering first a free-trade version of the model, and then considering the same model with the addition of a tariff on the imported good. We choose for our illustration the open economy model of Chapter 6, which includes public sector production, and allows for a choice of tax instruments. Before describing the experiment and its results, it is important to emphasise the assumptions that lie behind this model. It assumes constant returns to scale in production, and it incorporates the 'small country' assumption of fixed world prices; the government is assumed to balance its budget, and the balance of payments constraint is binding. Which of these assumptions is important when using the model to consider the effects of a tariff? The effects of protection can equally well be illustrated using a decreasing returns to scale model, and this exercise is suggested for the reader. The significance of the 'small country' assumption is discussed in the next section which demonstrates the changes in the model that result from making the 'large country' assumption, and comments on the implications for tariff policy. The assumption of general equilibrium, which is of course common to all our models, is the underlying reason why all the income constraints in the model must be satisfied; the point about the government budget and the balance of payments is repeated here because there is a common misconception that the imposition of a tariff can lead to a balance of payments disequilibrium. This is not correct in a real general equilibrium model of the kind discussed in this book. Explanations for balance of payments disequilibria must be sought elsewhere; one possible explanation is discussed in the next section.

For the computer experiment we use the program of Table 6.3. This program is first run in its existing form, with all the taxes initially set at zero, and the lump-sum income tax TY used to balance the public sector budget. For the second run of the program the import tariff is set exogenously at 0.1 by changing line 120 to read

120   LET TM = 0.1

The program is then run, using the same adjustment mechanism TY, and the consequences of protecting good 2 can then be seen by comparing the two sets of results.

These results in Table 7.2 are the antithesis of those discussed in the last section where we discussed the potential benefits from the introduction of free trade. By introducing an import tariff, some of the gains from trade are lost. The increased domestic price of good 2 encourages producers to switch to the production of the relatively capital intensive good 2 and the consumer's consumption of this good declines, now that it can no longer be freely imported at the

Table 7.2 Effects of a Protective Tariff

Free Trade Solution	Solution with import tariff
P1 = 1.4	P1 = 1.4
P2 = 1.6	P2 = 1.7
R = 0.80	R = 0.96
W = 0.80	W = 0.75
C1 = 0.79	C1 = 0.81
C2 = 0.69	C2 = 0.67
X1 = 1.24	X1 = 0.96
X2 = 0.16	X2 = 0.40
K1 = 0.54	K1 = 0.35
K2 = 0.16	K2 = 0.35
L1 = 1.64	L1 = 1.35
L2 = 0.16	L2 = 0.45
E = 0.45	E = 0.15
M = 0.39	M = 0.13
BP = 0	BP = 0
U = 0.742	U = 0.738

lower world price. The balance of trade reflects these changes in the economy; although the balance of payments still balances, the level of trade has dropped sharply. It is clear, and further computer experiments could show, that a higher level of import tariff could eliminate trade altogether.

It will be seen that the level of welfare, as measured by the value of U, has dropped with the introduction of a distorting tariff which eliminates some of the benefits of trade. There is, however, more to be said on this subject. It will be observed that with the change in the relative price of the two commodities, the factor prices have also been affected by the introduction of an import tax. With the increased production of the capital-intensive good, the rental on capital, R, has risen while W, the wage-rate, has dropped. Given the full employment assumption of the general equilibrium model, the same quantities of capital and labour are employed in both the pre-tariff and the post-tariff situation, so that the imposition of the tariff has increased the share of the national income going to capital at the expense of labour. The total remuneration of capital rises, while that of labour falls. This observation illustrates the Stolper-Samuelson theorem:

> The Stolper-Samuelson theorem demonstrates that the effects of a tariff are unambiguous within the context of the standard trade model. Following the Heckscher-Ohlin reasoning, we can say that a country exports the good which it produces primarily with the help of its abundant factor of production. A tariff will decrease production of exportables and lead to an increase in production of the import-competing good, and benefit the scarce factor — that used intensively in the import sector. Thus a tariff will benefit a country's scarce factor of production in an unambiguous fashion and cause the real income of the abundant factor to fall. (Sodersten 1980, p. 175)

In our one-consumer version of the two-sector model, the Stolper-Samuelson theorem does not have any welfare significance: as the single consumer is assumed to supply both factors of production, changes in their relative rates of remuneration are unimportant. If, however, there were two consumers in the model (see Section 7.7) and their initial endowments of the two factors differed, it is clear that one consumer might benefit at the expense of the other by the introduction of an import tariff, even though the community as a whole will suffer a welfare loss. In an extreme version of the two-consumer model (considered in 7.7), one consumer might own all the capital, and the other all the labour; in this situation, the Stolper-Samuelson theorem would have great relevance to the assessment of the welfare consequences of introducing an import tariff.

7.5   Monopolistic Export Markets

The open economy model presented in Chapter 5 and used for the analysis so far was based on the 'small country' assumption. In other words, it was assumed that the country in question had no influence over the world prices of the goods it exported or imported. In this section we examine the consequences of changing this assumption, and supposing that the country is a 'large country' in world trade. It is possible to assume that the country has a degree of monopoly in either its export or its import market. In the first case, the country would be faced by a downwards sloping demand curve for its exportable good, so that increasing the level of its exports would lower the price on the world market. In the second case, the assumption would be that the supply of imports was not infinitely elastic at a given world price, but that an increased quantity of imports would be associated with a higher price, as foreign suppliers moved up their marginal cost curves to meet the increased demand for their product. What would be the implications for the general equilibrium model of the open economy? If the economy had some monopoly power in both its export and its import market, the two world prices, P_{W1} and P_{W2} in our notation, would cease to be exogenous variables of the model. In our particular model where good 1 is the exportable, and good 2 the importable, P_{W1} would be determined by the level of exports, and P_{W2} by the level of imports. These variables would now be endogenous, and the two new equations required to complete the general equilibrium model would be

$$P_{W1} = P_{W1} E \qquad (7.3)$$
$$P_{W2} = P_{W2} M \qquad (7.4)$$

where it was assumed that there was an inverse relationship between the level of exports and the world price, and that there was a positive relationship between the level of imports and the world price.

It is more common to find monopolistic export markets than monopsonistic import markets (coffee from Brazil, cocoa from Ghana, oil from countries in the Middle East, are obvious examples), so in our numerical illustration we shall show how the open economy model of Chapter 5 can be adapted to incorporate equation (7.3) above, but we shall continue to assume that the world price of imports is exogenous to the model. For a numerical example, a specific assumption has to be made about form of the relationship described by (7.3). We will assume

$$PW1 = E^{-0.8} \qquad (7.5)$$

This equation has then to be added to the model of Table 5.2, and P_{W1} has to be added to the list of endogenous variables, and deleted from the list of exogenous variables. The computer program written to solve the open economy model of Table 5.2, given in Table 5.3, can now be adapted to make the world price of good 1 endogenous. Rather than listing a complete new program, we show how the program of Table 5.3 can be rapidly adapted by a few line changes. These changes are given in Table 7.3.

The changes in Table 7.3 are largely self-explanatory. PW1, previously an exogenous variable of the model, is now determined

Table 7.3 Changes to Computer Program of Table 5.2 Required to Incorporate Assumption of Monopolistic Export Market

---

```
10 REM OPEN ECONOMY MODEL WITH MONOPOLISTIC
   EXPORT MARKET
15 REM SUGGESTED INITIAL INPUT FOR PW1 = 1.4
40 INPUT "INITIAL VALUE FOR PW1? " PW1
260 LET E = PW1 ^ (−1.25)
271 IF ABS(C1+E−X1)<0.01 THEN GOTO 290
272 IF (C1+E)>X1 THEN LET PW1 = PW1+0.001
273 IF (C1+E)<X1 THEN LET PW1 = PW1−0.001
274 PRINT "PW1 = "PW1
275 GOTO 70
295 PRINT "PW1 = "PW1
```

---

endogenously: in the computer program, an initial value for PW1 is supplied; line 260 uses (7.5) to calculate the level of exports, E, associated with this value for PW1. Lines 271 – 275 are then added to the original program to search iteratively for the value of PW1 which ensures that the commodity balance equation for good 1 is satisfied. When this program is run, it will be seen that the equilibrium price for PW1 is 1.45, not very different from the value of 1 4 assumed exogenously in the earlier program, and suggested as an initial INPUT value at line 15.

Although the simple open economy model of Chapter 5 was used to demonstrate the way in which the assumption of a monopolistic export can be incorporated in the two-sector general equilibrium model, the model of Chapter 6, which includes a public sector, can be adapted in exactly the same way. The experimental reader will find that with the particular parameters chosen for these numerical examples, the consequence of making the world price of good 2 depend upon the level of the country's imports is to lead to specialisation, with domestic production of good 2 being eliminated. This result, which occurs for reasons discussed at the end of Chapter 5, is of course not necessary, and will not occur with a different choice of values for the exogenous factor endowments and/or different supply and demand functions.

The analysis of this section constitutes an important addition to the discussion of the effects of a tariff in the previous section. With the small country assumption the effect of a tax on trade is to lower the value of social welfare as measured by U in the computer programs. However, once a country is assumed to have elements of monopoly power in either its export or its import market, the possibility arises of exploiting these market imperfections by imposing taxes on the traded goods. While these taxes may lower welfare in the world as a whole, they can increase the level of social welfare for the country councerned by improving its terms of trade. Discussion in the international theory textbooks of optimal tariffs is concerned with the problem of setting these taxes at the level that maximises these potential gains. We do not consider this question here, but the interested reader who wishes to pursue this subject could adapt the numerical example of Chapter 6 to illustrate the welfare implications of such a tax policy by incorporating the appropriate conditions for optimisation in the model and writing the associated computer program.

7.6 The Public Sector Budget and the Balance of Payments

One of the points that was emphasised in the model of Chapter 6, which introduced the public sector into the two-good model, was that for general equilibrium the public sector had to balance its budget with any profits or losses from its productive activities counter-balanced by the imposition of subsidies or taxes. It is interesting to consider what would happen to the model if the government did *not* balance its budget. A full answer to this question cannot be provided within the context of a real general equilibrium model — one which deals with real variables only, and does not include a monetary sector. Nevertheless, an interesting computer experiment can be carried out which throws some light upon the so-called 'monetary theory of the balance of payments'.

For this experiment we use the numerical example of the model of Chapter 6, solved by the computer program given in Table 6.3. In that program public sector budget balance was achieved by an iteration in lines 430–520 which led to one of the taxes being adjusted until the government budget (PSB in the program) was not significantly different from zero. The condition that the balance of payments should not be significantly different from zero was not explicitly built into the computer program, but the constraint was satisfied by Walras' Law, when all the market clearing equations were satisfied and all the economic agents were on their budget constraints. If the government does not satisfy its budget constraint, what happens? The answer to this question can be discovered by deleting the iteration procedure of lines 430–520 from the program of Table 6.3. When this is done, and the program is run, it will be seen that the deficit on the public sector budget (PSB) is exactly reflected by the deficit on the balance of payments (BP). This observation provides some insight into the economic argument that deficits on the balance of payments are a consequence of the government's failure to balance its budget.

7.7   A Two-Consumer Economy

Some of the possible implications of including more than one consumer in the two-sector economy were briefly discussed in Section 7.2. In this section we suggest ways of introducing a second consumer into the model, and show how questions of distribution, eliminated by assumption in the one-consumer economy, arise when this modification is made.

We shall continue to use the assumption of utility maximisation to model consumer behaviour in the general equilibrium model, but with the introduction of a second consumer, the utility function of each must be considered. If there are two consumers A and B, their utility functions in the two-good model can be assumed to depend upon their respective levels of consumption of good 1 and good 2 which we denote C_{iA} and C_{iB}. We have therefore:

$$U_A = U_A(C_{1A},C_{2A}) \tag{7.6}$$
$$U_B = U_B(C_{1B},C_{2B}) \tag{7.7}$$

The demand functions for each consumer will be functions of income and the commodity prices:

$$C_{1A} = C_{1A}(Y_A,P_1,P_2) \tag{7.8}$$
$$C_{2A} = C_{2A}(Y_A,P_1,P_2) \tag{7.9}$$
$$C_{1B} = C_{1B}(Y_B,P_1,P_2) \tag{7.10}$$
$$C_{2B} = C_{2B}(Y_B,P_1,P_2) \tag{7.11}$$

where Y_A and Y_B will be determined by the relative prices of the system, and the initial ownership of the assets of the economy. These assets consist of the factors of production; and in a model with decreasing returns to scale they will also include a claim to the profits of the private sector firms. If we assume decreasing returns to scale

$$Y_A = rK_A + wL_A + \pi_{1A}\Pi_1 + \pi_{2A}\Pi_2 \qquad (7.12)$$
$$Y_B = rK_B + wL_B + \pi_{1B}\Pi_1 + \pi_{2B}\Pi_2 \qquad (7.13)$$

where K_A, K_B, L_A and L_B represent the respective endowments of capital and labour of each of the two individuals, and π_{iA} and π_{iB} represent the share of each in the profits of the two firms. With two sets of demands for each good C_1 and C_2 are defined by

$$C_1 = C_{1A} + C_{1B} \qquad (7.14)$$
$$C_2 = C_{2A} + C_{2B} \qquad (7.15)$$

For a numerical example of a two-person economy we return to the original simple closed economy model of Chapter 2. Any of the other models of the book could be adapted in a similar way, but the main points of interest that arise from the inclusion of a second consumer can be illustrated by this simple example. Before we can extend the model of Table 2.1 to incorporate a second consumer, the utility functions (7.6) and (7.7) have to be given a specific form. We assume that consumer A has the utility function used previously for the single consumer:

$$U_A = C_{1A}^{1/2}C_{2A}^{1/2} \qquad (7.16)$$

while the utility function of consumer B is described by

$$U_B = C_{1B}^{1/2}C_{2B}^{1/4} \qquad (7.17)$$

Each consumer maximises his utility subject to his budget constraint giving the four demand functions

$$C_{1A} = \frac{Y_A}{2P_1} \qquad (7.18)$$

$$C_{2A} = \frac{Y_A}{2P_2} \qquad (7.19)$$

$$C_{1B} = \frac{2Y_B}{3P_1} \qquad (7.20)$$

$$C_{2B} = \frac{Y}{3P_2} \qquad (7.21)$$

The incomes of the two consumers, Y_A and Y_B, cannot be specified without making *a priori* assumptions about the initial ownership of factors and assets in the two-person economy. In the context of a numerical example this means assigning values to the exogenous variables K_A, K_B, L_A, L_B, π_{iA} and π_{iB}. One interesting way of assigning these values is to assume that one of the two consumers is the 'capitalist' and one the 'worker'. We shall do this for our example, and we assume therefore that consumer A owns the entire capital stock, and receives the profits of the two firms, while consumer B owns and supplies all the labour in the economy. This implies the following set of values for the exogenous variables of the model, given the original assumptions about the size of the factor endowments:

$$
\begin{aligned}
K_A &= 0.8 \qquad K_B = 0 \\
L_A &= 0 \qquad\ L_B = 2.0 \\
\pi_{1A} &= \pi_{2A} = 1 \qquad \pi_{1B} = \pi_{2B} = 0
\end{aligned}
$$

With these values, the incomes of the two consumers are defined by

$$
\begin{aligned}
Y_A &= r(K_1+K_2) + \Pi_1 + \Pi_2 \qquad\qquad (7.22) \\
Y_B &= w(L_1+L_2) \qquad\qquad\qquad\qquad\quad (7.23)
\end{aligned}
$$

A numerical example, based on the model of Table 2.1, can now be constructed. The model of Chapter 2 consisted of 15 equations with 15 endogenous variables. With two consumers, the two demand equations of the original model, equations (1) and (2) in Table 2.1, will be replaced by the four demand equations (7.18) – (7.21); the original model equation (15), defining the single consumer's income, will be replaced by the two equations (7.22) and (7.23). If we now add the identities given as (7.14) and (7.15), the model will consist of 20 equations. What are the endogenous variables? We add C_{1A}, C_{2A}, C_{1B}, and C_{2B} to the original list, and replace the variable Y by the two variables Y_A and Y_B. This makes a total of 20 variables:

$$
C_1 \ C_2 \ C_{1A} \ C_{2A} \ C_{1B} \ C_{2B} \ X_1 \ X_2 \ K_1 \ K_2 \ L_1 \ L_2 \ P_1 \ P_2 \ w \ r \ \Pi_1 \ \Pi_2 \ Y_A \ Y_B
$$

With 20 equations in 20 unknowns a determinate solution is possible, and in Table 7.4 we list the changes that would be required to adapt the computer program of Table 2.3 to solve the two-consumer model. When this program is run, it will be seen that consumer A receives more income than consumer B (YA = 0.97, YB = 0.62) and consumes more of both goods. Because of the differing subjective values placed on goods 1 and 2 by the two consumers, consumer B spends far less of his income on good 2 than consumer A, and comparing the solution to this model with that of the original one-consumer model solved by Table 2.3, it will be seen that the resulting change in the pattern of total demand is reflected in a lower relative price for good 2. This change in demand has implications for the patterns of output and employ-

Table 7.4 Alterations to Computer Program of Table 2.3 Required for Two-Consumer Economy

---

10 REM TWO-CONSUMER ECONOMY CLOSED ECONOMY MODEL
20 REM SUGGESTED INPUT VALUES: P2=1.15, R=0.7, W=0.3
170 LET YA = R*(K1+K2)+PI1+PI2
175 LET YB = W*(L1+L2)
180 LET C1A = YA/(2*P1)
185 LET C1B = (2*YB)/(3*P1)
190 LET C2A = YA/(2*P2)
195 LET C2B = YB/(3*P2)
196 LET C1 = C1A+C1B
197 LET C2 = C2A+C2B
530 LET UA = C1A ^ 0.5*C2A ^ 0.5
540 LET UB = C1B ^ 0.5*C2B ^ 0.25
550 PRINT "CONSUMERS' INCOME, EXPENDITURE AND WELFARE"
560–630 PRINT statements for YA, YB, C1A, C2A, C1B, C2B, UA and UB

---

ment, and for factor earnings, which can be studied by comparing the general equilibrium solutions of the two models.

Further experiments can be carried out with this program. One useful exercise is to give the two consumers identical preferences, reflected in identical utility functions, and identical factor endowments. With the assumption that each consumer supplies exactly half of the quantities of capital and labour demanded by the two firms, it will be seen that the solution to the general equilibrium system is the same in the one-consumer model as in the two-consumer model. This experiment makes it quite clear what assumptions are being made when economists work with models containing only one representative consumer. Other experiments along similar lines are possible: different utility functions for *A* and *B* can be tried; different assumptions can be made about the ownership of assets in the economy. More complex models could be constructed by assuming that the two households *A* and *B* have individual factor supply functions. The approach that would fit into the neo-classical general equilibrium framework of this book would be to include factors supplied (with a negative sign) in the utility function, and then to assume that each individual equates the marginal gains from supplying factors with the marginal disutility incurred. This complicates the analysis, although no essentially new ideas are involved, and we do not pursue the subject here. We end, however, with a word of warning. When two or more consumers with different preference sets are included in the general equilibrium model, it will not always be possible to find a determinate solution to the system, and readers experimenting with many-consumer models should be aware of this potential problem.

Despite the limited nature of the computer experiments of this section, we have covered enough ground to show how problems of distribution can be handled within the two-sector framework. By making the amendments suggested in Table 7.4 to the open economy model of Chapter 5, or the governed economy model of Chapter 6, the effects of changing factor endowments, world prices, taxes or tariffs on the two consumers can be examined. The reader can show that, as emphasised earlier, a demonstration of welfare gains in the one-consumer economy must not be taken to imply that all consumers share in the gains. There are potential gains for all, but if there is no guarantee that gains will be redistributed between consumers, any given policy change may result in gains for some and losses for others.

7.8 Concluding Remarks

The computer experiments described in this chapter have had two purposes. The primary objective has been to show how computer experiments can be designed to illustrate some of the theorems of international trade theory in a way that brings out the full general equilibrium consequences of particular propositions. A subsidiary, more general, aim has been to show how the general equilibrium models of this book can be extended and adapted, and how numerical examples can be used to explore different areas of economic analysis. By using the suggestions of the different sections of the chapter, the interested reader can develop many variations of the two-sector model, and he or she is likely to find that each experiment suggests others, many of which throw an interesting light on the assumptions and assertions of economic theory.

References

Boadway, R.W. and Bruce, N. (1984) *Welfare Economics*, Basil Blackwell.

McKenzie, G. (1983) *Measuring Economic Welfare: New Methods*, Cambridge University Press.

Mishan, E.J. (1981) *Introduction to Normative Economics*, Oxford University Press.

Sodersten, B. (1980), *International Economics* (2nd edn), Macmillan.

8

BEYOND THE TWO-SECTOR MODEL

8.1 Introduction

The two-sector model of this book has so far been used for two purposes. In the first place, it has been used to show how a simple general equilibrium model can be constructed, using concepts and mathematical techniques familiar to most students of economics. By assuming that consumers maximise utility and producers maximise profits, and by using suitable functional forms to represent the tastes of the former and the technologies of the latter, simple models were developed in the early chapters of the book to demonstrate the way in which a perfectly competitive economy allocates its scarce resources. Two versions of a closed economy model were developed, one assuming decreasing returns to scale in production, and one assuming constant returns. In Chapter 5 the model was extended to include foreign trade, and Chapter 6 showed how a public sector could be integrated into the general equilibrium framework; with these additions to the model it was possible to examine some of the consequences of dropping the assumption of perfectly competitive markets throughout the economy, while preserving the general equilibrium nature of the system. The second object of the book has been to show how specific numerical examples of the general models can be used to illustrate the consequences of economic change for all agents and all markets in a two-sector economy. By using computer programs to solve these numerical examples, we have been able to illustrate a number of propositions from the theory of international trade. The intention has been to show how this new approach to learning economics makes it possible to stress the all-important linkages between markets and between sectors which are more difficult to convey by means of partial equilibrium analysis illustrated by diagrams.

In this last chapter we demonstrate a further advantage of this approach to the study of the two-sector model. The general principles which have been emphasised throughout the text can readily be employed to extend the analysis of general equilibrium systems to models with more than two sectors. We illustrate this assertion in Section 8.2 with a three-sector model, and in Section 8.3 with an n-sector model. In the remaining sections of this chapter we note some of the areas of economic analysis for which this book could serve as an introduction. Section 8.4 indicates some of the ways in which empirical use is made of general equilibrium models, and briefly discusses some criticisms of this approach to policy analysis. Section 8.5 suggests further theoretical avenues that could be explored.

8.2 Enlarging the Model

There are clearly many ways in which the very simple two-sector models of this book can be extended: more variables, endogenous and exogenous, can be added; more complex functional relationships can be used to develop numerical examples. A little has been said in earlier chapters about the possibility of using more complex relations to model demand and supply. The point has been made that the functions chosen must conform to the requirements of economic theory, but further discussion of these issues would require an excursion into econometrics, as reasons for preferring one utility function to another, or one production function to another, are likely to emerge from a consideration of the empirical evidence. This subject lies outside the scope of this text, and in this section we concentrate on the possibility of extending the models by adding more variables.

The basic model of this textbook has assumed two goods, two factors of production, and one consumer. The last section of the previous chapter briefly discussed the way in which additional consumers could be incorporated in the model and some of the consequences of enlarging the model in this way. We do not pursue this question in the present chapter, but we turn to the possibility of extending the model by increasing the number of commodities and/or the number of factors of production. It will be seen that extending the model in this way does not require the introduction of any new principles; while it is difficult to represent a three-good economy by the use of diagrams, and impossible if four or more goods are to be considered, the approach via general equilibrium models is immediate. For each new endogenous variable introduced, care must be exercised to see that the way in which the variable fits into the general equilibrium system is carefully defined, and the mathematical point noted in Chapter 1 has to be borne in mind: a system of equations will not, in general, have a solution unless there are as many equations as there are unknowns. Although the general principles of enlarging the model are straightforward, difficulties of ensuring that the model has a determinate solution may emerge in the open economy fixed price model if the number of goods is not equal to the number of factors. We discuss this point below, after showing how further goods and factors can be fitted into the general equilibrium framework.

Suppose that a third good, good 3, is to be added to any of the models of this book. What new variables and equations will be required? There will be an additional variable C_3 defined by a demand equation; and there will be an additional variable X_3 to represent the supply of the commodity. The way in which this variable fits into the general equilibrium system will be dictated by the particular assumption made about the nature of the returns to scale in production. If we denote the capital and labour used to produce the third good by K_3 and L_3, then with the decreasing returns to scale model of Chapter 1 there will be a supply function to define X_3, factor demand functions defining K_3 and L_3, and a fourth variable Π_3 defined by the firm's profit function. (This variable Π_3 must be incorporated in the consumer's income.) With the constant returns to scale model of Chapter 3, there will be a unit cost equation, per unit factor demands, k_3 and l_3, and equations defining these variables in terms of X_3, K_3 and L_3. Finally, in both versions, a new commodity balance equation will be required for the market for good 3. This equation will determine the equilibrium price for the good, P_3. In all, six new variables (C_3, X_3, P_3, K_3, L_3, Π_3) and six new equations will be added to the model if decreasing returns to scale are assumed; and seven variables (C_3, X_3, P_3, k_3, l_3, K_3, L_3) and seven equations if constant returns to scale are assumed.

The inclusion of a third factor of production would proceed along similar lines. Assume that the third factor is represented by N ('natural resources'), and its price by h. The demand for this factor will then be given by the sum of the demands of the individual firms; if we preserve the simplifying assumptions of the models of this book about the nature of factor supplies, the supply will be given by the fixed factor endowment $N^\star$. The new endogenous variables of the model will be given by N_i, where i is the number of firms employing the factor, and the price h. The variables N_i will be defined by the factor demand functions of the individual firms; the precise way in which the use of the factor is incorporated in the production relations of the firm will, as above, depend upon whether decreasing or constant returns to scale are assumed. The value of the variable h will be determined by the factor market clearing condition.

When all the relative prices of the (one-consumer) general equilibrium system are market determined, there is in principle no reason why a unique solution cannot be found, provided that the model is properly specified. There are, however, likely to be problems in open economy models which assume constant returns to scale in production, and fixed world prices. The nature of this problem was discussed in Section 5.2: in the two-good, two-factor economy with constant returns to scale the two unit cost equations are

$$P_1 = rk_1 + wl_1 \tag{8.1}$$
$$P_2 = rk_2 + wl_2 \tag{8.2}$$

where the per unit factor demands k_i and l_i are functions of the factor prices r and w. With the 'small country' assumption P_1 and P_2 are determined by world price levels, and the above two equations are then a pair of simultaneous equations in the variables r and w. The solution to the two equations determines the unique values of r and w compatible with fixed world prices. We discussed in Section 5.3 the implications of these fixed prices for the nature of the full employment solution of the two-sector model, and showed in Section 5.4 that for both goods to be domestically produced in an open economy the initial endowments must fall within the cone of diversification. Here we are concerned with the problem that arises if a third traded good produced with constant returns to scale is introduced into the model without increasing the number of factors of production. A third unit cost equation will be added to the model:

$$P_3 = rk_3 + wl_3 \tag{8.3}$$

and with three equations in two unknowns the system is over-determined and it will not in general be possible to find solutions for r and w.

There are several ways in which the model can be re-specified in order to escape from this dilemma. A third factor could be incorporated in the model, in which case there would be three unit cost equations in three unknowns and a solution is possible. The assumption of constant returns to scale could be dropped, and with decreasing returns to scale and supply functions for each firm a solution could be found. Finally, the assumption of fixed world prices could be abandoned; if the assumption of infinite elasticities for export demand and import supply is not made, then world prices become endogenous in the manner discussed in Section 7.5. This is the solution adopted in the n-good model discussed in the following section. It should be noted that the over-determination problem arises in the three-good, two-factor model when all three goods are assumed to be traded internationally. An interesting class of models, one example of which is given below, assumes three goods and two factors, but also assumes that one of the goods is non-traded. In this case, the problem is again resolved: if good 3, for example, is assumed non-traded, then even with constant returns to scale and the 'small country' assumption, a solution to the three unit cost equations can be found. The values of r and w will be found from equations (8.1) and (8.2), and substituting these values in (8.3) will determine the price of the non-traded good 3. The model is still a fixed-price model, but it is not over-determined.

The above discussion relates to the problems that can arise with three goods and two factors of production. What would happen if there were two goods and three factors? Again the problems arise in the open economy constant returns to scale versions of the model when fixed world prices are assumed. If the per unit demand for factor N by firm i is represented by n_i, and, as above, h is used to denote the price of N, then the unit cost equations for the two firms will be given by

$$P_1 = rk_1 + wl_1 + hn_1 \qquad (8.4)$$
$$P_2 = rk_2 + wl_2 + hn_2 \qquad (8.5)$$

where k_i, l_i, and n_i will be functions of the three factor prices r, w, and h. Two equations are not enough to determine unique values for three unknowns; in this case there will be an infinite number of possible solutions. The problem of more factors than goods is in general less serious than the converse problem discussed earlier; partly because a plurality of solutions is less intractable than no solution to a system of equations, but more importantly, because in any empirical use of a general equilibrium model there is likely to be a far larger number of goods than primary factors, even if extensive sub-divisions of the categories of 'labour', 'capital' and 'natural resources' is made.

Although we have confined ourselves to a discussion of the ways in which one more good or one more factor could be added to the two-sector model, it is clear that the discussion generalises. More goods, and more factors can be added indefinitely; the procedures used and the potential problems involved can all be demonstrated in a three-sector model. Readers will be able to think of variations on the theme: one possibility is to make the third good a 'public good' supplied by the government to the consumer free of charge. The quantity supplied could be treated as an exogenous variable of the model, but the consequences for public sector levels of employment and the public sector budget would have to be taken account of in the general equilibrium system, and losses incurred by the government would have to be recouped by the imposition of taxes.

We conclude this section by presenting a particular three-good model which serves as an example of how to extend the two-sector model of earlier chapters, and also demonstrates how some new exogenous variables can be incorporated in the general equilibrium system. The model presented in Table 8.1 includes three goods produced in both the public and the private sector with a decreasing returns to scale technology; goods 1 and 2 are traded, and good 3 is non-traded. The third good has been incorporated in the general equilibrium framework of our earlier models by adding the various endogenous variables and the equations required in the manner discussed above. The model includes a number of taxes: there is a commodity tax t_{C3} on the non-traded good so that the consumer price Q_3 differs from the producer price P_3; t_E is a subsidy on the exportable good and t_M is an import tariff so that in this model the domestic price differs from the world price of both the traded goods. As in earlier models, these commodity taxes are assumed to be per unit taxes, but the model of Table 8.1 also includes an example of a proportionate tax: this is a tax on profits, assumed to be levied at a uniform rate t_Π, on all three firms. All of these taxes are assumed to be set exogenously. The one endogenous tax is the lump-sum tax (or subsidy) t_Y which is set at the level required to balance the public sector budget.

A new exogenous variable, not previously encountered, is to be found in the balance of payments equation (28). This is the variable d, defined as a net capital inflow from abroad, and denominated in foreign currency. The effect of an exogenous capital inflow (which might for example represent a foreign aid grant) is two-fold. In the first place, it redefines the balance of payments constraint. The value of imports no longer has to be exactly equal to the value of exports, but can exceed it by the amount d. In the second place, the capital inflow d constitutes an addition to the income generated within the economy and must therefore be incorporated in one of the income equations. In this model it has been included in the income of the public sector by adding the term Fd. The other variables of the model are all familiar from the earlier models of the text.

The model presented in Table 8.1 does not in itself have any particular significance. It is, however, of considerable interest as a

Table 8.1 A Three-Good, Two-Factor General Equilibrium Model of an Open Economy with Tax Distortions

COMMODITY MARKETS

Demand	$C_1 = C_1(P_1, P_2, Q_3, Y)$	(1)
	$C_2 = C_2(P_1, P_2, Q_3, Y)$	(2)
	$C_3 = C_3(P_1, P_2, Q_3, Y)$	(3)
Supply	$X_1 = X_1(P_1, w, r)$	(4)
	$X_2 = X_2(P_2, w, r)$	(5)
	$X_3 = X_3(P_3, w, r)$	(6)
Market clearing	$C_1 = X_1 + G_1 - E$	(7)
	$C_2 = X_2 + G_2 + M$	(8)
	$C_3 = X_3 + G_3$	(9)
Prices	$Q_3 = P_3 + t_{C3}$	(10)
	$P_1 = F_{S1} - t_E$	(11)
	$P_2 = F_{S2} + t_M$	(12)

FACTOR MARKETS

Demand	$K_1 = K_1(X_1, w, r)$	(13)
	$K_2 = K_2(X_2, w, r)$	(14)
	$K_3 = K_3(X_3, w, r)$	(15)
	$L_1 = L_1(X_1, w, r)$	(16)
	$L_2 = L_2(X_2, w, r)$	(17)
	$L_3 = L_3(X_3, w, r)$	(18)
Market clearing	$K_1 + K_2 + K_3 + Kg = K^\star$	(19)
	$L_1 + L_2 + L_3 + Lg = L^\star$	(20)

DOMESTIC SECTOR
BUDGET CONSTRAINTS

Consumer

$$Y = rK^\star + wL^\star + \Sigma\Pi_i(1-t_\Pi) - t_Y$$
$$i = 1,2,3 \tag{21}$$

Private sector
firms

$$\Pi_1 = P_1X_1 - rK_1 - wL_1 \tag{22}$$
$$\Pi_2 = P_2X_2 - rK_2 - wL_2 \tag{23}$$
$$\Pi_3 = P_3X_3 - rK_3 - wL_3 \tag{24}$$

Public sector

$$G = \Sigma P_iG_i - wLg - rKg \tag{25}$$
$$T = t_EE + t_MM + t_{C3}C_3$$
$$+ t_\Pi\Sigma\Pi_i + t_Y$$
$$i = 1,2,3 \tag{26}$$
$$G + T + Fd = 0 \tag{27}$$

BALANCE OF PAYMENTS
CONSTRAINT

$$P_{W1}E - P_{W2}M + d = 0 \tag{28}$$

There are 14 exogenous variables
$$P_{W1},P_{W2},K^\star,L^\star,G_1,G_2,G_3,Kg,Lg,t_E,t_M,t_{C3},t_\pi,d$$
and 28 endogenous variables
$$C_1,C_2,C_3,X_1,X_2,X_3,M_1,E_2,F,p_1,p_2,p_3,q_3,w,r,$$
$$L_1,L_2,L_3,K_1,K_2,K_3,Y,\Pi_1,\Pi_2,\Pi_3,G,T,T_Y$$

representative of a class of models which includes both traded and non-traded goods. Many of the interesting questions in applied economics arise because policies have differing effects on the markets for traded and non-traded goods, and these questions cannot readily be handled by the diagrammatic treatment appropriate to the two-sector model. A device sometimes used (and referred to as the 'Australian model') is to reduce the three-good model to a two-good model by combining the exportable and the importable good into one composite category, which is then referred to as the 'traded good'. This can, however, be confusing, and we would argue that a much more satisfactory approach is by means of a three-good general equilibrium model. Three-sector models, of which a number of examples can be found in the advanced literature, are a very powerful theoretical tool for examining the effects of policies which have different effects on the relative price of traded and non-traded goods. One of the advantages of the approach of this book which uses formal general equilibrium models is that the same approach can be used for analysing economies with and without a non-traded good. A numerical example of the three-good model of Table 8.1 is not included here, but such an example could readily be constructed and used for experiment by any student who has followed the analysis of the earlier chapters.

In the next section we show that an *n*-sector model is also readily accessible to anyone familiar with the approach to two-sector models of this book, and we choose for our example a model which, unlike the models considered so far, has been used for an empirical investigation.

8.3   An *n*-Sector Model Used for Policy Analysis

In this section we discuss an example of an empirical use of a general equilibrium model to be found in an article by Robin Boadway and John Treddenick published in the *Canadian Journal of Economics* in 1978, and entitled 'A General Equilibrium Computation of the Effects of the Canadian Tariff Structure'. The authors based their paper on a neo-classical general equilibrium model of an open economy which could be solved explicitly for a solution with or without tariffs on imported goods. Data from the Canadian economy were used, and the effects of the Canadian tariff structure were analysed by comparing the solutions to the model with and without tariffs on the various industries considered. We discuss the model in some detail, partly because it is interesting in its own right, but also because it shows that enough material has been covered in this book to enable the reader to understand the construction and use of a full-scale general equilibrium model used for policy analysis in a particular economy.

The basic model employed by Boadway and Treddenick was an open economy model of an economy with constant returns to scale in the industrial sector. The production functions included two primary inputs, capital and labour, and inter-industry flows. For the primary inputs the authors experimented with both Cobb-Douglas and CES production functions, while inter-industry flows were allowed to enter either in fixed proportions (as in our two-commodity model in Chapter 4, Section 4.3) or in variable proportions according to a Cobb-Douglas technology. There are *n* industries in the model and the equations of the general equilibrium system are developed in the opening section of the paper in a way which will be fully comprehensible to any reader who has worked his way through the two-commodity models of this book. The model is summarised in a footnote on pp. 429–430 and this summary is reproduced below. The functions are presented as general, not specific, relations, as the authors experiment with different functional forms for their empirical analysis.

Table 8.2 The Model Used by Boadway and Treddenick to Investigate the Effects of the Canadian Tariff Structure

$L \;\; = \Sigma l_i(w,r)X_i$	$i = 1, \ldots ,n$
$K \;\; = \Sigma k_i(w,r)X_i$	$i = 1, \ldots ,n$
$X_i \;\; = \Sigma a_{ij}X_j + Q_i(Y,p) + E_i(w,r,e) - M_i(w,r,e)$	$i = 1, \ldots ,n$
$p_i \;\; = \Sigma a_{ji}p_j + wl_i(w,r) + rk_i(w,r)$	$i = 1, \ldots ,n$
$\Sigma p_iE_i(w,r,e) - \Sigma p_i(1-t^M)M_i(w,r,e) = 0$	$i = 1, \ldots ,n$
$Y = Y(w,r,p_i,e)$	$i = 1, \ldots ,n$

where
  X_i is the output of industry i
  L is the (exogenously) given supply of labour
  K is the (exogenously) given supply of capital
  w is the wage rate
  r is the rental on capital
  l_i is the unit demand for labour in industry i
  k_i is the unit demand for capital in industry i
  Q_i is the demand for good i
  Y is consumer income
  p_i is the domestic price of good i
  E_i is exports of good i
  M_i is imports of good i
  e is the exchange rate
  t^M_i is the rate of tariff on imports of good i

It will be seen that the notation used in the model of Table 8.2 is very similar to that used for the two-sector models of this book. The only differences are that Q_i is used for the demand for good i, rather than C_i; and e, not F, is used to represent the exchange rate. The first two sets of equations in the model of Table 8.2 give the market clearing conditions for labour and capital. The third set of equations summarises the commodity balance equations; and the fourth set of equations give the unit cost equations for this constant returns to scale model. The last two equations define the two income constraints for the model: the balance of payments condition (expressed here in terms of domestic, rather than world prices) and the equation describing the single representative consumer's income. A feature of the model, which the reader will also be able to relate to the analysis of this text, is the use of export demand and import supply functions with less than infinite elasticities. Infinite elasticities are ruled out on the grounds that world prices would exogenously fix domestic prices and the system would be over-determined with only two primary factors and n commodities.

Boadway and Treddenick comment on their model 'There are $2n+4$ equations in $2n+4$ unknowns (X_i, p_i, w, r, e, Y). By Walras's Law one equation may be dropped. Also the system is homogenous of degree zero in p, w, r and e. Therefore we can arbitrarily select $r = 1$ to normalise prices. That leaves $2n + 3$ independent equations in $2n + 3$ relative prices.' The model is solved by finding the equilibrium wage rate from which the values of all the other variables can be determined. A comparison with the computer program of Table 4.4 will show that this procedure is almost identical to the method used to solve the two-sector input-output model: in that program the other factor price w was normalised at unity and the capital market clearing condition was used as the basis for the iteration procedure.

The model has been reproduced in full to show the reader of this book that although our exposition has concentrated on two-commodity models, the general ideas developed make the extension to the n-commodity model straightforward. This will be still more obvious to the reader who looks at the original Boadway and Treddenick paper to see the equations of the model developed, prior to the summary reproduced here.

After their presentation of the basic n-commodity model, Boadway and Treddenick discuss briefly some modifications required for them to be able to use their Canadian input-output data in the model. These modifications include inter-industry wage rate differentials, commodity and corporation taxes, and a respecification of the treatment of imports which allows for foreign goods being imperfect substitutes for domestic products.

Two versions of the general equilibrium model, one using 56 industry categories and the other aggregating the data into 16 industry groups, were then solved with and without import tariffs. The authors found that the qualitative conclusions reached were similar for a wide range of alternative assumptions about the structure of the model: only differences in export demand elasticities proved significant. Numerical results for one set of assumptions are presented in four tables showing the consequences of eliminating tariffs and other tax distortions. Effects on relative factor prices, the exchange rate, and welfare are reported: as in the present text, changes in welfare are measured by a Cobb-Douglas utility function which rises and falls in value with the imposition and removal of tariffs and other distortionary taxes. Changes in industry outputs, factor use, final demand and trade are also analysed.

The conclusions reached by Boadway and Treddenick were unexpected. They found that the Canadian tariff structure, far from encouraging Canadian manufacturing, appeared to discriminate against primary and manufacturing industries, and favoured non-traded tertiary industries. Furthermore, other expected effects relating the changes in welfare and changes in the wage-rental ratio proved insignificant. The authors stress that the results of their computations cannot be considered definitive, and they point to other modifications of their model that might be desirable for further investigations, but the study as a whole is a very interesting example of an empirical use of a general equilibrium model.

8.4 The Empirical Use of General Equilibrium Models

The example of the previous section showed how a general equilibrium model can be used for policy analysis. By constructing a model of the Canadian economy which could be solved by a computer, Boadway and Treddenick were able to consider the consequences of tariff protection by solving the model with and without the imposition of import tariffs. The similarity of this procedure to the hypothetical 'experiments' of this book will be obvious. The principal additional requirements for empirical analysis are statistical and econometric data to portray the structure of an actual economy, and perhaps a larger computer!

Many of the empirical applications of general equilibrium models have been concerned with the analysis of trade policy. One example of a general equilibrium model devised to measure the effects of trade policies on a national basis is the ORANI model of the Australian economy. Australia is unusual in that tariff protection has for a long time been a live political issue and, partly as a result of this political interest, economists in Australia have taken a very active interest in the economic effects of tariffs. The first systematic attempt to measure these effects was made by the Bridgen committee of enquiry into the Australian tariff in the 1920s. The work of this committee was discussed and its analysis extended by Corden (1957) in a paper which instigated much further work on the effects of tariff protection. All these investigations were partial equilibrium in character and it was not until the introduction of computers, and the collection of an enormous amount of data, that it was possible to set up a full general equilibrium model to analyse the problem. The ORANI model was the result, and various versions of this model have been employed both to analyse the consequences of tariffs on an economy-wide basis, and as a taking-off point for other studies of the Australian economy. A small scale version of the ORANI model can be found in Scarf and Shoven (1984), Chapter 12.

Another area in which general equilibrium models have been found useful is in the field of development planning. Models of varying degrees of sophistication underlie planning procedures used in both developed and less developed countries. Readers interested in the use of general equilibrium models for development policy could look at Dervis, de Melo and Robinson (1982). Among other topics the authors discuss the application of input-output accounts to the study of the sources of structural change in a group of eight countries: Korea, Taiwan, Japan, Turkey, Mexico, Columbia, Israel, and Norway — countries at very different levels of *per capita* income which have followed a wide range of development policies. Part II of their book, entitled 'Computable General Equilibrium Models' contains more difficult material than that in the present text, but much of the discussion could be followed by anyone interested in seeing how the analysis of this book has to be developed to build a full-scale model of an actual economy. The authors demonstrate their approach with reference to a model of the Turkish economy which is used to study the serious foreign exchange crisis that developed in that country in 1977.

The use of general equilibrium models for policy analysis is open to criticism in a number of respects. The reader may well have queried the full-employment assumption of the general equilibrium model when used for empirical investigations, and other assumptions taken from the competitive market model are likely to seem unconvincing when applied to the real world. It should be emphasised that the use of a general equilibrium model does not imply that *all* the assumptions of perfect competition have been made; on the contrary, the examples given above make it clear that one of the important uses of such models is in simulating the effects of tax distortions on trade and welfare. However, the assumption that the behaviour of firms can be described in terms of the profit-maximising, competitive textbook market model, and the assumption that prices in all markets including factor markets, will constantly be iterating towards an equilibrium price which ensures a market clearing solution, are aspects of the general equilibrium approach which appear to offer poor descriptions of the real world. We briefly consider these two criticisms.

An implication of the assumption of perfect competition in the theory of the firm is that firms are price-takers: no individual firm can influence the price at which it sells its product. Furthermore, the theory implies that each profit-maximising firm will set marginal cost equal to price, and that changes in the market price will lead the firm to respond by moving along its marginal cost curve. It has been argued that both of these predictions are at variance with the empirical evidence. The real world, it is argued, is characterised by large multinational companies and diversified oligopolies which have considerable influence over the prices of their products. In this type of market situation there is no presumption that marginal cost will be equated to price, even if firms are presumed to be profit-maximisers (an assumption also open to dispute). There is considerable evidence to contradict the marginalist pricing theory that underlies general equilibrium models. Many studies show that prices are typically set by firms on the basis of a mark-up on unit costs and not by reference to marginal costs. Cronin (1985) cites studies from a number of countries including Australia, United States, Sweden, Germany, United Kingdom and other OECD countries, which have as a common strand in their results 'a rejection of the hypothesis that prices in the industrial sector increase substantially during upswings by movements along rising short-run marginal cost curves.'

Does such evidence from the real world invalidate the use of general equilibrium models? In the short run it may be doubted whether the assumption of the perfectly competitive profit-maximising firm is plausible as a description of the industrial framework in a modern economy. The question is whether the observations of the previous paragraph about the behaviour of firms in the short run (even if correct) invalidate the assumptions of general equilibrium theory in the long run. Much of the literature referred to above is concerned with pricing policy in the trade cycle, and the reaction to short-run changes in demand. To argue that firms maximise profits in the long run is not necessarily inconsistent with evidence that they do not adjust instantly to short-run changes in the demand for their products. Profit-maximisation remains a powerful and plausible assumption in a competitive environment because a firm that does not make profits in the long run does not survive.

The question, however, remains as to whether present-day firms can be said to operate in a competitive environment. The evidence is that within economies imperfect markets are the rule, rather than the exception, for most industrial production. To the extent that markets are dominated by a few large-scale producers, the neo-classical general equilibrium model of market behaviour will provide a poor description of the sectors concerned. Two responses are likely to be made by the proponent of the use of general equilibrium models: one is that although producers in domestic markets are often price-makers, not price-takers as in the competitive model, the existence of international trade means that for many goods there is an alternative source of supply available at world prices which are not normally (with the 'small country' assumption) under domestic control. If the economy is a reasonably open one, producers must take these foreign prices into account, and the assumptions underlying the firms' behaviour in the general equilibrium model look more convincing. On more theoretical grounds, it can be argued that no economic model (even one based on empirical data) will provide a perfect description of the real world; the purpose of such models, as argued by Friedman (1953), is to make predictions. Models should be evaluated by the accuracy of their predictions, rather than by the realism of their assumptions.

The presumption of full employment appears more difficult to defend on the above lines, as an implication of general equilibrium models is that their solutions will be characterised by full employment, whereas in actual economies unemployment is widely observed. It is important when discussing this issue to be clear exactly what is assumed in a general equilibrium model. In the simplified models of our text, the full employment condition was built into the solution of the model by the simple expedient of assuming that the firms' demands for capital and labour were always equated to the initial (fixed) factor endowments. Full employment would also have resulted if factor supply functions, fully specified in terms of the relative prices of the system, had been used. The assumption is that markets will clear because prices are fully flexible both upwards and downwards; this implies that all those who wish to work at the prevailing wage rate will be able to do so: there will be no involuntary unemployment. The predictions of the model are therefore compatible with the observation that if prices are not fully flexible, markets will not necessarily clear. The predictions of the model are not, however, compatible with the belief that even if prices are flexible, there will be unemployment. This is the issue which Keynes addressed in the 1930s, and his work has given rise to a different class of models which may be generally classified as 'Keynesian'. In these models, unemployment is caused by the deficiency of aggregate demand, and (unlike the real general equilibrium models with which this book has been concerned) Keynesian models try to integrate both real and monetary variables in their analysis.

An alternative approach to modelling market behaviour in macro-models has been the development of fix-price, quantity-constraint models, often referred to as 'disequilibrium' models. These models, which also have their intellectual origins in the work of Keynes, are based on the hypothesis that prices are rigid in the short run; they consider the ways in which economic agents respond to perceived quantity constraints in any given market, and the consequences for the other markets of the economy. The reader interested in this approach could look at Cuddington, Johansson and Lofgren (1984). The introductory chapters of this book describe the theoretical background to disequilibrium modelling, and the subsequent analysis makes extensive use of two-sector models.

The use of these different types of model for policy analysis is comparatively recent. The problems raised by trying to devise realistic models which can be used to describe actual economies and can provide a basis for policy prescriptions are great and challenging, and no formulations at present satisfy all the requirements of both the theoretician and the policy maker. A survey of the relative merits and demerits of each type of model cannot be attempted here, but we conclude with a quotation from Scarf and Shoven (1984) who write that in spite of its imperfections 'there are no competing formulations that . . . provide the flexibility and conceptual wealth of the general equilibrium model'.

8.5   General Equilibrium Models and Economic Theory

The simple general equilibrium models of this book can be thought of as providing a starting point for two types of analytic inquiry. One use of the models has appeared in this text: even the simplest two- and three-good models can be used as a vehicle for teaching about and for learning economic theory. The most obvious branch of economics to be treated in this way, and the one which has been explored in Chapters 5 and 7, is international trade theory. The two-sector model has been widely used for teaching trade theory and we have argued that the new approach of this book can contribute another dimension to this way of presenting the subject.

Trade theory is not the only branch of analysis to use simple general equilibrium models as an expository tool. Students proceeding to graduate work in economics will find that the theory of cost-benefit analysis, too, makes extensive use of such models. Examples of two-good, three-good, and n-good models are all to be found in the journal literature on this subject. The theory of optimal taxation is another field where the use of simple general equilibrium models has proved valuable. A well-known paper by Dasgupta and Stiglitz (1974) used a one-consumer, n-commodity general equilibrium model to discuss rules for both project appraisal and optimal taxation, and their analysis has led to a number of similar contributions in both fields. With the addition of factor supply functions, and some changes in the assumptions made about the taxes imposed, the three-good model of Section 8.2 (built on the foundations of the analysis of the preceeding chapters of this book) could be interpreted as a small-scale version of the Dasgupta and Stiglitz model. We would argue that time spent mastering the way in which the very simple models of this book are constructed would be a good investment for understanding the journal literature in these various fields.

A quite different use for the analysis of this book is to see it as a preliminary to the study of general equilibrium theory. The theory of general equilibrium is one of the most advanced and sophisticated areas of economic analysis, and it is not possible in this introductory textbook to do more than draw attention to the problem originally identified by Walras, and the subject of extensive research by such mathematical economists as Arrow, Debreu and others, as to whether, and under what conditions, a unique and stable solution will exist for models of general equilibrium.

The starting point for this line of enquiry was the observation that the Walrasian system is characterised by a large number of independent agents who enter the market either as consumers or producers, and who base their decision about what quantities to buy or sell on the prevailing set of market prices. All agents are assumed to take prices as given, and no one individual has any control over market prices. There is no reason to suppose that for any arbitrary set of prices the quantity demanded will equal the quantity supplied; in general, markets are likely to be characterised by excess stocks, or by running down of stocks in the face of excess supply or demand. This observation leads to two related questions. In the first place, will there be a unique set of equilibrium prices that ensures all markets clear? In the second place, what is the economic process that leads to the equilibrium solution? If all agents take prices as given, what causes them to change?

Walras considered two lines of argument. The first was based on the view that a solution can be expected for a system in which the number of endogenous variables is equal to the number of independent equations. This assertion has, however, been shown to be incomplete without further analysis. To deal with the puzzling question of what causes prices to move towards their market clearing values, Walras introduced the idea of an 'auctioneer' who called out prices for each market, initially at random, but subsequently reducing prices for markets in which excess demand was observed, and raising prices in markets where there was excess supply. This process was known as 'tatonnement', and the reader will see that the iteration process in the computer programs written to solve the general equilibrium models of this book is an exact reproduction of Walras' process of 'tatonnement'.

Recent work in mathematical economics has conclusively demonstrated that general equilibrium models are consistent — that there exists a set of prices that will equate supply and demand for all the markets of the economy. The fixed-point theorems on which the existence proofs are based do not, however, provide information about how the market clearing prices are to be calculated, and further research work has been devoted to devising methods of solving general equilibrium systems by mathematical procedures known as algorithms. A number of such algorithms now exist. From an economic point of view these solution procedures still leave something to be desired, for they are typically not based on a model of market behaviour, showing prices responding to excess supply and demand. Professor Hahn (1982) concluded in a recent survey of the stability properties of general equilibrium models that 'while some special models exist, we shall have to conclude that we still lack a satisfactory descriptive theory of the invisible hand'.

It is not the purpose of this book to teach general equilibrium theory. Analysis of the existence and the nature of solutions to general equilibrium systems requires a knowledge of both economics and mathematics that lies well beyond the level of this book. The simple general equilibrium models of this text by-pass many of the problems of general equilibrium theory. By assuming a single-consumer economy, and by making specific assumptions about the shapes of the utility functions and production functions that rule out the possibility of non-convexities or discontinuities, we have generated models for which the market-clearing iterative process leads to a unique and stable solution. It must be emphasised that such models constitute a special case. Nevertheless, understanding the concepts involved in the construction of these specific examples of general equilibrium models provides a basis for approaching the wider questions of general equilibrium theory.

8.6 Conclusion

We have tried in this last chapter of the book to suggest some ways in which the two-sector model can be extended and used for both empirical and theoretical purposes. We have shown that the approach of the book is one that can easily be adapted to construct models of three or more sectors, and we considered in Section 8.3 a particular n-commodity model which has been used for an empirical study. The last two sections of the chapter have necessarily been very superficial surveys of the work being done and the problems being tackled in the construction and use of large-scale empirical general equilibrium models, and in the theoretical field of general equilibrium analysis. We hope, however, that some readers of this book may feel encouraged to continue as

Hills peep o'er hills, and Alps on Alps arise!

References

Boadway, R. and Treddenick, J. (1978) 'A general equilibrium computation of the effects of the Canadian tariff structure', *Canadian Journal of Economics*, Vol. XI, pp. 424–46.

Corden, W. (1957) 'The calculation of the cost of protection', *Economic Record*, Vol. 34, pp. 331–346.

Cronin, M.R. (1985) 'The ORANI model in short-run mode; theory versus observations', *Australian Economic Papers*, Vol. 24, pp. 24–53.

Cuddington, J.T., Johansson, P. and Lofgren, K. (1984) *Disequilibrium Macroeconomics in Open Economies*, Basil Blackwell.

Dasgupta, P. and Stiglitz, J.E. (1974) 'Benefit-cost analysis and trade policies', *Journal of Political Economy*, Vol. 82, pp. 1–33.

Dervis, K., de Melo, J. and Robinson, S. (1982) *General Equilibrium Models for Development Policy*, A World Bank research publication, Cambridge University Press.

Friedman, M. (1953) 'The methodology of positive economics', *Essays in Positive Economics*, University of Chicago Press.

Hahn, F. (1982) 'Stability', in Arrow, K.J. and Intriligator, M.D. (eds) *Handbook of Mathematical Economics*, North-Holland, Vol. II, Ch. 16.

Scarf, H.E. and Shoven, J.B. (1984) (eds) *Applied General Equilibrium Analysis*, Cambridge University Press.

SUGGESTIONS FOR FURTHER READING

A number of books have already been suggested for further reading on specific topics and have been referenced at the end of the relevant chapters. The books listed here are textbooks grouped by subject for those who wish to pursue any particular aspect of this text. Roughly speaking, the references under the heading 'Mathematics' cover the material of Chapters 1–4; and the references under 'International Trade' are for those who wish to pursue some of the issues considered in Chapters 5 and 7. The books included under the heading of 'General Equilibrium' complement or extend the analysis of the present text as a whole. The list is not meant to be in any way comprehensive.

Mathematics

The formal mathematics of this text has deliberately been kept to a minimum. Elementary calculus and the first-order conditions for a constrained optimum are the only requirements for the derivation of the equations of the general equilibrium models in Chapters 1 – 4. These topics are covered in almost all textbooks on introductory mathematics for students of economics. At an undergraduate level, a concise introduction which includes economic applications of the subjects covered is:

Glass, J. Colin (1980) *An Introduction to Mathematical Methods in Economics*, McGraw-Hill.

A more comprehensive, but very clear, treatment which includes the second-order conditions for constrained optima is to be found in:

Chiang, A. (1984) *Fundamental Methods of Mathematical Economics* (3rd edn), McGraw-Hill.

An interesting discussion of these topics, which starts at an elementary level but which also considers the limitations of the methods employed in this text, is provided by:

Birchenhall, C. and Grout, P. (1984) *Mathematics for Modern Economics*, Philip Allan.

For the input-output analysis of Chapters 3 and 4, there is an elementary introduction in:

Holden, K. and Pearson, A.W. (1983) *Introductory Mathematics for Economics* (2nd edn), Macmillan.

And a classic exposition is to be found in:

Dorfman, R., Samuelson, P.A. and Solow, R.M. (1958) *Linear Programming and Economic Analysis*, McGraw-Hill.

International Trade Theory

There are many excellent introductions to this subject. Two textbooks recommended for undergraduates are:

Sodersten, B. (1980) *International Economics* (2nd edn), Macmillan.

Lindert, P.H. (1986) *International Economics* (8th edn), Irwin.

And at a slightly more advanced level:

Bhagwati, J.N. and Srinivasan, T.N. (1983) *Lectures on International Trade*, MIT Press.

At the graduate level, the following textbook, based on a general equilibrium approach, is strongly recommended:

Dixit, A. and Norman, V. (1980) *Theory of International Trade*, Cambridge University Press.

General Equilibrium

As noted in the Preface to this book, general equilibrium models are not often treated at an elementary level. An early exception to this statement is to be found in a very clear introduction to the subject, written in the days when economics students were not expected to know any calculus:

Phelps Brown, E.H. (1936) *The Framework of the Pricing System,* Chapman and Hall.

A more recent work at an introductory level is:

Simpson, D. (1975) *General Equilibrium Analysis,* Basil Blackwell.

A full treatment of the two-sector model which complements and extends the analysis of the present text is to be found in:

Baldry, J.C. (1980) *General Equilibrium Analysis, An Introduction to the Two-Sector Model,* Croom Helm.

Most intermediate microeconomic textbooks include chapters on general equilibrium. See, for example:

Layard, P.R.G. and Walters, A.A. (1978) *Microeconomic Theory,* McGraw-Hill.

Gravelle, H. and Rees, R., (1981) *Microeconomics,* Longman.

To proceed further in this subject, more mathematics is required. An introduction for graduates or advanced undergraduates is:

Allingham, M. (1975) *General Equilibrium,* John Wiley and Sons.

And a lively discussion is provided in:

Weintraub, E.R. (1985) *General Equilibrium Analysis, Studies in Appraisal,* Cambridge University Press.

For a short introduction to the subject by an outstanding economist in the field, students could read the lecture given by Professor

Arrow when he received the Nobel Prize in Economic Science in 1972. It is reprinted in:

Arrow, K.J. (1974) 'General economic equilibrium: purpose, analytic techniques, collective choice', *American Economic Review,* Vol. 64, pp. 253–72.

NOTES